The Knock-Knock Book

If I Hear God Knocking, Do You Think I Should Answer?

By

Judith Burhans

© 2001 by Judith Burhans. All rights reserved.

No part of this book may be reproduced, stored in a retrieval system, or transmitted by any means, electronic, mechanical, photocopying, recording, or otherwise, without written permission from the author.

ISBN: 0-75965-063-2

This book is printed on acid free paper.

TABLE OF CONTENTS

INTRODUCING 1

PART I GETTING STARTED   Judy Burhans 5

    Brick Knocking or God Knocking?   Internet 9

PART II FRIENDS 13

    Reflections   Sandy McCutcheon 13

    My Friend/My Sister   Judy Burhans 22

PART III ANSWERS TO PRAYERS 29

    It's Just Not Fair   Anonymous Author 30

    Kicking (Cigarette) Butts   Kay Bradburn 37

    Meet Benjamin   Susan Sadler 43

    ...A Time to Move, A Time to Stay Put...

        Kay Bradburn 48

    Say What?   Anonymous Author 54

PART IV POSITION NEEDED: MOM   Internet 60

    How to Become a Mom Without Really

    Trying (Or, Unexpected Gifts)   Judy Burhans 63

Josh's Grasp	Sandy McCutcheon	78
Above And Beyond	Sandy McCutcheon	82

PART V THE MOM BEFORE ME 90

The Images of Mother	Internet	90
The Spittin' Image of Jean	Judy Burhans	92
Meet My Mom and My Dad and My Mom and My Dad	Kay Bradburn	103

PART VI KNOCKS, WHISPERS AND OTHER ATTENTION GETTERS 109

Full Circle	Susan Sadler	111
Silence Isn't Always Golden	Kay Bradburn	114
When Faith Is Bruised	Karen Zecher	117
And God Said...	Kay Bradburn	124
Let Go - Let God	Judy Burhans	129

The Knock-Knock Book
If I Hear God Knocking, Do You Think I Should Answer?

INTRODUCING

Kay is one of my 'precious jewel' friends — so refined that no matter what hare-brained idea I've come up with, she calmly says, "Yes, Judy. Whatever you say." I'm NOW finding out what she really means when she says that! Read on...

JB

****

When my good friend Judy first asked me if I'd be interested in writing some things for a book called Knock-Knock, I said, "What do you mean by 'knock-knock'? Like a knock-knock joke? Like the hard knocks life hands us? Like a knock on the door? What do you mean, Judy?"

And Judy's reply, as I recall, went something like this: "Yes."

Well, naturally, with guidance like this, I immediately sat down and started burning up the keyboard! No…in fact, I stalled Judy for weeks. She kept emailing me and calling me, saying, "So how are you doing with your knock-knocks?" And I kept coming up with reasons I hadn't started yet.

One day as we sat at my kitchen table drinking coffee, I confessed that I just didn't quite understand the concept. I still didn't get what she meant by

Judith Burhans

"Knock-Knock." But that day as we chatted, I began to see that I should interpret "Knock-Knock" however God was guiding me to understand it.

Well, with breakthrough understanding like that, you'd think that now I rushed straight to my desk and started burning up the keyboard. But no…in fact, now all those alibis I'd been handing Judy for my not getting started seemed to really be happening.

Suddenly I really was way too busy for writing something "extra." I couldn't even find time to keep up with my paper grading and my housework; how was I going to find time to see where God was leading me on the whole Knock-Knock venture?

All of my classes at the university were suddenly over-enrolled, each additional student contributing stacks more to an already huge load of paper grading. My father-in-law, in a nursing home in North Carolina, took a bad turn. As part of a checkup, my husband had a stress test that showed "abnormalities." My daughter and son-in-law, who were building a house in a neighboring town, needed support during a problem time with their contractor. It was suddenly almost time for Lent, and Judy, the Minister of Music at our church, kept pulling out more and more and more new music for the adult choir and the ensemble, the two groups I sing in. A good friend who was diagnosed with cancer had her esophagus removed, and I wanted to do what I could to support her husband. Etc., etc., etc.

Then suddenly one morning – as I write this, it was this very morning, in fact – in the midst of my preparing to drive into town and teach my classes, I faintly heard, "Knock-Knock." Busily showering and shampooing, I paused only for a moment before getting on with my primping.

"Knock-Knock!!" it came again.

This time I stopped and thought, Oh, no…not now, God! I've got to get to school! And I went on to dry and curl my hair.

"KNOCK-KNOCK!!!" again, and this time more insistently. So I threw on some clothes, ran to my desk, and this time…YES! I started to write! The words came easily now. Where before I hadn't known what to say or how to begin, suddenly I could see that one of my "Knock-Knocks" was, in fact, underway even as I typed.

What was God's message with this Knock-Knock? I think it was some or all of the following: "Listen and heed My command" "Ask not how; just follow Me, and I will show you the way." "Be still and know that I am God."

Kay Bradburn

Judith Burhans

****

"Be still and know that I am God; I will be exalted among the nations, I will be exalted in the earth. The Lord Almighty is with us; the God of Jacob is our fortress." (Psalm 46:10-11, NIV)

PART I

GETTING STARTED

I turn on the computer and once IT boots up and is ready, IT and I have a staring contest. Any thoughts I had had prior to turning IT on are usually all gone, but the consolation in that is this: I win the staring contest – IT blinks.

****

I sat down at this computer to put down some thoughts that had crossed my mind right after church, but before the computer had warmed up, three people came into my office to ask various and pertinent questions. Now that I'm warmed up and looking at a screen, the thoughts have vanished. Knock-knock! It's a good example of the title of this book. Every day, we all have little knock-knocks that occur; sometimes we answer them, sometimes we push them aside, sometimes we ignore them, sometimes we don't even hear them!

I won't go into detail about how I've never written anything like this before, but now that I've dropped that little detail, I'll ask for your patience

Judith Burhans

as you and I plow through this together and see what comes out at the end. I'll also tell you up front that for my qualifications, I don't have an abused childhood lurking in my past. I don't have a problem with drugs or alcohol clouding my days. (Heaven knows, I can cloud up my day just fine without any help from anything else!) I've never been locked up in a mental institution against my will – or even WITH my will – so if you're reading this book specifically for those little tidbits to see how I handled them, sorry. I haven't been there or done that. In fact, sometimes I wonder just how much God really thinks I could handle, if put to the test, and if He knows I'd fail the test miserably. (I didn't say I SHOULDN'T be locked up!)

That may be pushing the love of God a little bit TOO far – I don't really want to suffer in any way, shape or form. It seems, though, that those who can tell the most heart-breaking stories, or cause the most tears to fall, are those who have been in such deep darkness that when they "see the light" and have victory over the pain and suffering, their joy is so great! My life and experiences seem to pale, in comparison.

So, what makes me think I can write a book about women, specifically mothers, and some of the experiences we live through, if I haven't had all the hard knocks? Well, here's why I think I can give it a shot, anyway:

1: I'm a woman.

2: I'm a mother.

3: I've had experiences, not all of them pleasant.

4: I've heard some knocks and missed others.

5: I need attitude adjustments every day.

6: I've been through (more than once, even) the "doom and gloom, not coming out of this room" syndrome.

7: If I have something that will work for you, then I'd like to share it. We all know that directions don't come with the kids/husbands/activities-of-daily-living, but maybe knowing that others are alive and trying will give you the push you need to answer that knock-knock of life and deal with it.

Speaking of sharing, since I am a firm believer in getting as much support around me as possible when doing something that other people will see/hear/read, I asked for, and got, the support of a few wonderful women I know, and they have all contributed to the authorship of this publication. We all come from different backgrounds and different walks of life, but we

Judith Burhans

all have knock-knocks, so kick back, put the kids in bed or send them to their grandmother's house, turn off the phones, play some "Point of Grace" in the background, and enjoy our rendition of "The Knock-Knock Book."

Judy Burhans

The Knock-Knock Book
If I Hear God Knocking, Do You Think I Should Answer?

BRICK KNOCKING or GOD KNOCKING?

You've heard the expression, "It was like running into a brick wall," haven't you? This usually describes a situation where no matter how hard you tried, you could not break through the barrier that had been put in place, for whatever reason it had been put in place. I think sometimes God must feel like He's running into a brick wall with us. So many times, in so many ways, He gives us opportunities to be His servants, to show others by our actions that we are His, and so many times, we present our brick walls to Him.

Following is a story I found on the Internet, and the original storyteller is unknown to me. However, the story seemed to be exactly what I wanted to give you to show an illustration of what I'm really trying to say. Read on!

JB

****

A young executive was driving his brand new Jaguar in an area where there were usually several children playing in the street. He thought he saw something darting out from between parked cars and slowed down. As his car passed, no children appeared. Instead, a brick smashed into the Jag's side door. He slammed on the brakes and spun the Jag back to the spot from where the brick had been thrown.

Judith Burhans

He jumped out of the car, grabbed some kid and pushed him up against a parked car shouting, "What was that all about and who are you? Just what the heck are you doing?" Building up a head of steam, he went on. "That's a new car and that brick you threw is going to cost a lot of money. Why did you do it?"

"Please, mister, please. I'm sorry, I didn't know what else to do!" pleaded the youngster. "I threw the brick because no one else would stop." Tears were dripping down the boy's chin as he pointed around the parked car. "It's my brother," he said. "He rolled off the curb and fell out of his wheelchair and I can't lift him up." Sobbing, the boy asked the executive, "Would you please help me get him back into his wheelchair? He's hurt and he's too heavy for me."

Moved beyond words, the driver tried to swallow the rapidly swelling lump in his throat. He lifted the young man back into the wheelchair and took out his handkerchief and wiped the scrapes and cuts, checking to see that everything was going to be okay. "Thank you and God bless you," the grateful child said to him.

The man then watched the little boy push his brother down the sidewalk toward their home. It was a long walk back to his Jaguar - a long, slow walk.

He never did repair the side door. He kept the dent to remind him not to go through life so fast that someone had to throw a brick to get his attention.

Internet

****

God whispers in your soul and speaks to your heart. Sometimes when you don't have time to listen, He has to throw a "brick" at you. It's your choice: Listen to the whisper - or wait for the brick.

Judith Burhans

PART II

FRIENDS

Friends are a bonus that God gives us in this lifetime – the sunshine that we need when the rest of our day has been a bunch of rainfall; the rainbow that promises us a smile and a lift; or a shoulder for a tear – a rare and precious jewel. When we're given friends who want only what is best for us and who support us, then we've been given a wonderful gift, indeed! God tells us to pick our friends wisely, and while there are many examples in the Bible that show what a BAD friend can cause us, there's a special one that sums up a friend for me:

"If one falls down, his friend can help him up. But pity the man who falls and has no one to help him up!" (Ecclesiastes 4:10, NIV)

JB

****

REFLECTIONS

We counted down for days, our excitement building as we looked forward to a wonderful Mother's Day gift from our husbands. Bob, Rod, and David had all agreed they could handle the home front with children, meals, and hectic schedules for four days so that we three could enjoy some hard-earned R&R on the sugar-white beaches of the Gulf of Mexico.

We sang all the way to the beach and when we arrived close to midnight, we ran knee-deep into the waves, arms outstretched toward the heavens and heads flung back while we breathed in the salt air and laughed with the joyous, free feeling. We unloaded the van and then sat on our third floor balcony and marveled at the crescent moon reflecting on the water. Ah! Three full days to relax!

During those days, we did everything we wanted to do, when we wanted to do it, and didn't worry about each other. We awoke by our inner alarm clocks, at different times. We walked for hours exploring the area, danced on the beach, swam in the pool, read books, went to the movies, and shopped. But the most memorable part of the trip was the wonderful silences as we lay on the sand soaking it all in: salty air, soft waves, crabs scurrying, gulls screeching, pelicans swooping, all of nature serenading us as the sun baked our bones and started to heal our wounds.

You see, these four days were a gift to us, not just to frolic in the sand, but to spend private time dealing with issues we each had to face head on. My personal pain was one that most mothers dread when their youngest child reaches maturity and prepares to leave home; Sue was trying to balance a career with caring for her husband and children and helping her mother cope with her own aging mother; and Karen was learning to live with a terrible loss.

Our daughter was 23 years old and already living outside our household. Our 17-year-old son was about to graduate from high school and leave for college far away. I was facing empty-nest syndrome, and I kept wondering how my role was going to change. How dull would our house be without the energy of a teenager? How would Bob and I relate again as a couple after 24 years of having our children around us? Scenes from my life as a mother kept floating to the surface of my mind now: birthing, breast feeding, tying shoelaces, cutting hot dogs into bite-size chunks, getting caught skipping the last few pages of bedtime stories when I thought they were asleep, taking them to Sunday School, riding bikes with them, rushing to ballet and soccer practices, seeing them off to dances, meeting numerous boyfriends and girlfriends over the years, hosting sleepovers, and now watching our youngest graduate from high school. What exactly was my role as a mother of two grown children? Was I still considered a Mom? Did they need me any more?

Judith Burhans

As usual when I'm at the beach, I awoke very early and walked toward the expected sunrise, preparing to photograph the beginning of a new day. As the pinks, yellows, and blues streaked across the sky and introduced the small orange glow peeking above the sand dunes, my tears began to flow. I wrote the words "Amazing Grace" in the sand and sang that familiar song as I caught the promise of a new day on film. Just as morning was breaking, a great weight lifted from me when I suddenly realized something – God was showing me that my life was full of colors and changes just like the sunrise. I will always be the mother of my children. I can always love them and pray for them no matter how far they are from my side. Each day of our lives is different and no matter how that day ends, we have the promise of a new sunrise through our Creator. We can sleep late and miss the sunrise while knowing it's there or we can watch for it and be awestruck by its beauty.

After seeing my answers in the sunrise, I turned around and started walking back down the beach. I saw a woman far away in silhouette, feet planted in the sand, waves lapping at her ankles, arms full of something, and her head bowed low. As I got closer, I realized the woman was Sue. Obviously, she too had gotten up to watch the beginning of the new day.

Sue was working hard and doing a fine job of balancing husband and children with professional duties along with helping her mother make decisions regarding her maternal grandmother, who was beginning to lose moments in time. Sue was committed to her nursing profession, but she deeply loved her husband and her children, Anna and Alan, who were involved in everything from soccer to karate to church choir. But along with fulfilling her professional, wifely, and motherly duties, she wanted to help as her mother struggled through the tough time of watching her own mother become more and more fragile. Realizing that this grandmother whom she loved would only be with her a short time longer, Sue wanted to spend as much time as possible with her. And all of these demands were creating enormous stress in Sue's life. "How can I balance my time, Lord?" she prayed. "There are so many demands for every minute of my day. How can I cover the important things in life with my family amidst this hectic schedule?"

As I drew closer to Sue that morning on the beach, I saw that tears were streaming down her face. It took a moment for her to clear her voice to say, "I was thinking of my family and especially Anna and Alan. They're growing up so fast. I wanted them to know I thought about them this weekend, so I really wanted to take them some shells from the beach. But why is it I never find shells? I kept looking and watching but only found tiny shells. I prayed that He would show some to me that were worthy of taking home to share this wonderful weekend with them. And as soon as I prayed, I turned the bend in the beach and there they were – eight of the largest shells I've ever seen outside of a store! I know now something that I need to always remember and I need to share it with my family. I need to teach them to always ask Him for help, no matter how small it may seem. He's there to walk with us every step of the way." Sue's realization was very moving, and both of us cried joyful tears and hummed "Amazing Grace" as we went back along the beach to find Karen.

Karen hadn't left the room at sunrise but she had gotten up to sit on the balcony and think quiet thoughts while looking down on the beach. She saw two stingrays in the water very close to shore, gliding along together up and down the current. It seemed appropriate that she saw these deadly rays in view of the horrible sting she had recently suffered. She was the mother of Megan, age two, and had given birth to Will just a few short weeks before this trip. He was gorgeous, 8 1/2 pounds, 21 inches long, head full of dark hair, and within a few hours of his birth he already had the stubborn streak of his paternal grandfather for whom he was named. Karen's pregnancy had been normal. The nursery was decorated with Noah's Ark figures, and friends and neighbors were pleased that Karen and David were having a son. Everything seemed perfect.

But Will had trouble when he slipped into the birth canal, and the umbilical cord wrapped around his neck at the last moment. Minutes later when he was born, the oxygen supply had been interrupted and Will was in trouble. We saw him in the neonatal intensive care unit and he looked so healthy compared to the preemies that were so tiny. Surely if babies can live at 2-1/2 pounds these days, Will would be fine. But he wasn't. He lived only until the next day.

Now Karen was going through her physical recovery from the childbirth, experiencing the emotional roller coaster of changing hormones, and coping with the all-encompassing grief that she and David shared. She and David, along with their close-knit family, their friends and entire congregation at church, neighbors, and even the merchants they dealt with were devastated. But Karen and David stayed solid in their faith in the Lord. We all have to contend with life and death, but the death of a child seems by far the worst pain. With the rough storm that Karen was (and is) enduring, she knows there is a promise of new sunrises, and it was about this that she thought as she gazed down on the ocean that morning. She knows that Christ is her Savior, and she and David have a very personal relationship with Him. They know He is beside them and helps them through their days. They have a most beautiful daughter and they praise His Holy Name.

Sue showed us the shells she had collected. All of them were perfect, except for one. It had a broken place on it, but instead of throwing it away, Sue had turned it over and found that in spite of its imperfection on one side, it was actually the most beautiful and unique of the shells God had shown her. This shell made Sue think of Will, and she shared that with Karen.

We spent the last few minutes of our beach stay that Mother's Day morning in the living room with the patio door open, the breeze creating a backdrop for our prayers, scripture, and song. And we ended our worship time with a final prayer of thanks: "Thank you, Lord, for giving to us the beauty you have shown us in your creative works. Thank you for our wonderful husbands that gave us no guilt for being away this weekend and for being such great sports with the extra work they had to do in our absence. Thank you for allowing us the privilege of being mothers and please show us how to help our children grow to know you. Thank you for our mothers (and mother-in-laws) for their understanding that we couldn't be there to share this special day with them. Thank you for the gift of Christian friends. Thank you."

Many miles and much laughter later, as we neared home, God gave us one final gift to end our trip. As we crossed the bridge over the Tennessee River, He treated us to an explosive sunset with all the colors of the sunsets at the beach. It was almost as if He was saying, "Remember, I'm still with you. Peace be to you, girlfriends."

Sandy McCutcheon

****

"Peace I leave with you; my peace I give you. I do not give to you as the world gives. Do not let your hearts be troubled and do not be afraid." (John 14:27, NIV)

Judith Burhans

MY FRIEND/MY SISTER

Have you ever been asked the question, "How many friends do you have?" I remember a teacher asking me that once, a long time ago, and I can remember thinking, "Oh-oh." That's it - just "oh-oh" - because at certain points in life, more friends mean more popularity, right? And everyone wants to be popular – or at least, "acceptable." So when everyone started giving the teacher answers to that million-dollar question, the numbers increased as more kids answered the question. I guess the one who answered "151" was counting every person she'd ever known since kindergarten, plus relatives, brothers and sisters she fought with, all of her pets, and the names of people she'd seen in the post office on the "Wanted" posters. Well, maybe it was the phone book. Anyway, being a pastor's daughter, I could never come up with more than three names, max. And I just knew that if I'd lie and say "10," I'd probably be caught in that lie and have to give up those 10 names. So I'd just mumble my "threefriendsthat'salll'vegot" answer and hope no one was paying attention.

Little did I know that to be able to say I had three friends, who are REALLY friends, was a gold mine and nothing to be ashamed of. While I was growing up, my family moved four times to different congregations, and four years at any one spot was about the maximum amount of time we spent anywhere. I learned early that I wasn't one of the "rooted" ones who would live somewhere for most of my life, and if I wanted to keep in touch with any of these kids, I would have to write letters.

As an adult, I married a military career man, and life continued to be a series of moves, only this time, 18 to 24 months was about the longest average stop in one place. When this is life, there are two ways to cope: either don't get involved and don't make any friends because you know you're going to be leaving soon, anyway, or jump right in and start – time's a-wasting! Most of the time, I jumped.

Now, jumping down south in Georgia is a lot different from jumping in Illinois, where I grew up. For one thing, the people talk funny down here, there's not much snow (and what little there is, closes roads!), and air conditioning seems to be THE basic element of life. However, if you can learn to take a coat shopping with you and readjust the sound waves in your ears, you can do it. Finding a friend or three helps, too.

To get to the point of my story, I need to let you know that whenever we move, the first place I look for is the church, and if it has a parochial school,

Judith Burhans

so much the better. In Georgia, Lutheran churches are sparse, but I found one, with a school, so that's where we headed. We began attending services there, and one child started school there. Our second school year, we needed to find a group of people to be on the PTL board (Parent-Teacher League, the Lutheran version of PTA). I'm NOT a leader, and sitting in on long, boring meetings is not my thing, so I was not volunteering to be An Anything on this board. However, I was asked to be on a committee of two to find five members who would be on the board, and that, I figured, I could do – pass the buck on to someone else!

Enter Cynthia. Cynthia was an airline stewardess who was in the air a lot of the time, and even when she was on the ground, she never really grounded to a halt. She had three children, two of whom went to this school and thus, our first connection. We had a mutual friend who had been on the PTL board the year before, but our mutual friend's husband said that our mutual friend was NOT going to be doing boards any more; she was going to stay home and be a mother. A mutual-friend-sit-at-home-do-nothing-mother. Fine. Cynthia and I, who didn't really know each other except through Angie, our mutual-do-nothing-friend, could deal with this. All we had to do was find five willing people out of a pool of 125 unsuspecting adults, and our working relationship would be done. Piece of cake.

Four hours, 125 phone calls, and 123 turn-downs later, I called Cynthia.

"Cynthia, this is Judy. Had any takers to be president/vice-president/secretary/treasurer/parliamentarian?"

"Nope. How about you?"

"Not a single one, except this one lady said she'd consider being the parliamentarian if we couldn't find anyone else."

"Put her name in the slot – we've got one! What's a parliamentarian do, anyway?"

"I don't know, probably just sits there. You know, the other one who just sits there is the vice-president. Do you think Jim would let Angie 'unsit-at-home' one night a month and just sit at the board meeting as a vice-president? She still wouldn't have to DO anything."

"Good idea. You want to call Jim and ask if she can?"

"Not me, lady! You've known them longer than I have – you call and ask him. Besides, he doesn't like me much – Angie spends too much time with me, he says."

"Well, I don't know...Maybe we can think of someone else."

"Right. Did you miss calling anyone on your list?"

"No."

"Then I think we're stuck. You know, I wouldn't mind being the secretary – she doesn't have to do any talking – but I sure wouldn't want to be the president. I'd have to cancel all the meetings due to cold feet."

"Well, I was just thinking that I wouldn't want to be the secretary, but I wouldn't mind being the president – all they have to do is talk."

"So, Cynthia, if you were the president, and I were the secretary, and if Angie could be the vice-president as long as you don't miss any meetings and make Angie DO anything, the Parliamentarian has already accepted, and the treasurer is glued to her chair and won't give up the position, anyway, then we're done trying to get people to sit on the board. How's that sound?"

"You want to call Jim?"

Thus began a friendship that probably wouldn't have ever occurred except through a committee of two. I knew it was a true friendship, though, one night when we were attending a progressive dinner. For anyone not acquainted with a progressive dinner, it's a meal that is spread out over any number of people's houses, and you go to one person's house for appetizers, another person's house for soups, another person's house for the entrée, etc.

Cynthia had the dessert house, and she asked me if I'd come with her a little earlier than everyone else was going to show up to help get the coffee perking, since she didn't drink coffee and didn't want to make a bad pot. I said sure, let's go!

Off we went, about seven miles to her house, talking the whole way about nothing in particular. Since I had never been to her house before, I was checking out the neighborhood, ooh-ing and aah-ing at flowers and trees growing in her yard. Walking in the front door, I checked out everything there, too. Then, I glanced into one room off to the right, and there was this woman with a little girl, working on some cookies and cakes.

I poked Cynthia and whispered, "Cynthia, there's a black lady in your house."

Cynthia looked at me to see whether I was serious; then she cracked up and said, "Judy, that's my *sister*."

FYI: Neither Cynthia nor her sister is adopted...Knock-Knock!

Judy Burhans

****

"You are all sons of God through faith in Christ Jesus, for all of you who were baptized into Christ have clothed yourselves with Christ. There is neither Jew nor Greek,

Judith Burhans

slave nor free, male nor female, for you are all one in Christ Jesus. If you belong to Christ, then you are Abraham's seed, and heirs according to the promise." (Galatians 3:26-29, NIV)

PART III

ANSWERS TO PRAYERS

Sometimes — well, actually, make that most of the time — "things" happen in our lives and we just don't have a clue as to why they happened. Seeing the "cause and effect" is a typical human solution to explain phenomena that might otherwise keep us up all night trying to figure them out (This is about to get deep — hang in here with me!). In other words, we can understand that when a child leaves the ice cream container sitting on the counter instead of putting it in the freezer, we have melted blobs of ice milk all over the counter. Taken one step further, we can even understand that while once that particular counter top was clean and life was good, it is now full of ants celebrating, and more ants on the way. We may not like it, but we do understand it. It's all part of creation and God's plan, right? Part of that "cause and effect" equation, right? Well, maybe.

So, how do we explain the death of a child, or the termination of a pregnancy before its time? How do we "cause and effect" an accident that takes away the use of a child's arms or legs, or a meningitis that paralyzes for life? How do we accept a divorce of someone whom we perceived as a "perfect" couple, or an affair and the subsequent devastation? Not quite as simple as the ice cream and the ants to explain, is it? Probably our first response, after the shock and pain, is, "It's just not fair!"

JB

****

IT'S JUST NOT FAIR

Babies are supposed to be an easy thing to have – just get married, do whatcha gotta do, and voila! Pregnant! Right? After years and years of having to take daily temperatures, marking them down on my basal temp chart, swallowing one to three pills for five days in a row, and calling my husband and saying, "It's TIME, dear – right NOW," I have come to this conclusion: the only ones who can ever get pregnant by just "doing it" are those who are having illicit sex – you know, the kind you're NOT supposed to have until you're married. Just how fair is that?

From a totally jaundiced point of view, it starts to seem like there are a lot of people who don't need kids, but who keep having them, anyway; there are people who can't take care of the kids they have, but don't seem to know how not to have kids; and there are people who need to have their kids taken away from them because they abuse them. And, of course, when you're trying so desperately to have just one baby, EVERYONE around you is pregnant or delivering, and it starts to become a painful experience just to leave your house.

My first child was born three years after I'd been married. Up until that point, having a baby was not a goal – if it happened, it happened; if it didn't, it didn't. In other words, I didn't know what I was missing until this baby was born! After five more years of "natural" living (if it happens, it happens; let it happen, let it happen) and nothing happening (no pregnancy), I began the first of many trips to the doctor's office for some help.

My second pregnancy occurred after only three months of Clomid and temperature charts – a record for me, I was to find out later. However, pregnant I was, and pregnant I would be – for five whole months.

It just so happened that at that time, I was working in a radiology department as the office manager. One day when the crew in the radiology side of the house was lacking for anything to do, they asked me if I wanted to have an ultrasound – on the house. Always one for a bargain, and this one was free, I said yes, of course. So, here we go – monitor ready, gel warmed up, transducer set to roll across the abdomen – and the only thing I hear after all the preliminary talking and silly jokes to make me relax is...silence. There was not a sound in the room from the ultrasound techs, the nurse or from me. Ever so quietly, the radiologist was called into the lab, and he looked at the monitor, had some x-rays taken, and then called me into his office.

The choices given to me at that time were these: I could either go through the pregnancy until it terminated itself, at which time I would deliver a non-viable (non-living) fetus, or I could terminate the pregnancy sooner, and the result would be the same – a non-viable fetal delivery. The choices were not acceptable to me, the outcome of either choice was not desirable, and come to think of it, these weren't even choices! Why was God doing this to me? What had I done to deserve this happening?

I cried – Oh, to God, I cried – and to God I screamed and got mad and carried on like a demented person without reason – which I was. Why was He doing this? Couldn't He change the outcome? Didn't He know I'd be a great mother if He'd just let me have this baby?

Obviously, He didn't know, or maybe He didn't care. Maybe He wasn't even listening. I just knew there was something happening to me that I had no control over, nothing was going to change just because I didn't like it, and God was gone.

The next couple of days, up to a week, were probably the most horrible days I had ever lived through. Nobody could say anything that was helpful, nobody could give me any hope or peace, and absolutely nobody even had the foggiest idea what was going on with me and this knowledge that I had to live with. And then, my body started its own abortion, and I continued to die, all alone. I went to the hospital and was admitted, but it wasn't to a labor and delivery room that I was admitted, nor was I put anywhere near the nursery. I don't know exactly where I was – all I know is that I was ostracized. My doctor came and talked to me, told me basically what to expect and said everything would be over in 24 hours, and said I should call him if I needed anything.

The night began. My cramping and contractions started and continued. My water broke; my gown was soaked. My sister came to stay with me, and she was the one who found new bed sheets for my bed and a dry gown for my body – not the nurses who were supposed to be working that shift. When my sister had to leave for a few hours to sleep, it was a cleaning lady with her mop and bucket who came into my room, found me crying, got me a wet cloth for my face, held my hand, and talked to me for over an hour until she had to get back to her job.

Before daybreak, I called for a nurse, told her I thought I was about to have this delivery, and she brought me a bedpan – and left. I found out later that she never even called my doctor to let him know what was happening to me. When he came through for his rounds at 8:00 AM, I had already aborted the baby three hours earlier. I will give him credit – he sent the nurse packing – but by then, I didn't really care. I was numb. I had seen the "non-viable" fetus, and it was beautiful. He was a little boy, perfectly formed from his little toenails up to his nose and baby blue eyes. Beyond his forehead, he had no skull formation; thus, part of the reason for the eventual non-viability, I guess. It seemed such a waste – and so unfair! So, what was God's plan in this pain?

Three years later, I was working as a labor and delivery nurse when we got the word in our unit that a woman had been brought up to the GYN floor for a therapeutic abortion in the morning for a "non-viable" fetus. Knock-knock? I don't think so, God. I'm NOT the one to go talk to this woman. Do You think I have no feelings? Two hours went by, then another one, and I could stand the knocking no longer. I told my supervisor where I was going, and off I went to find this woman, in whose mind I knew exactly what was going on. I had been there; I was back – with her. I held her hand as she lay in the dark room, told her of my "baby" who wasn't here, and told her the pain of losing a baby, for whatever reason, would eventually fade – I hoped – but the memory of the baby lost would stay with her for a long, long time – probably forever, but I wasn't to forever, yet.

I'm not sure what else I told her, but I remember saying that if she needed me at any time during the rest of the night, I could come back and be there. She asked for me the next day, after it was all over for her – and the healing just trying to begin – and we just sat there and mourned together.

To this day, I still don't have an answer, or an explanation, for God not letting me have that little boy to love. I sit here and write this, and my tears are falling as fresh as if the loss occurred only yesterday. I wonder if the woman that I talked to has let go and gone on, and how she "grew" from the experience. Maybe God stretched me so I could have empathy for others suffering; maybe He wants me to bring His love and comfort to them because I know how alone one can be without Him. Maybe He wanted me to learn to trust His judgment and to know that He is always in control, whether I am or not, and that He loves me, even when I am VERY

Judith Burhans

unlovable! And maybe His blessings for me to love are going to come in packages other than the way I expect them to come.

Author Anonymous

****

"For I know the plans I have for you,' declares the Lord, 'plans to prosper you and not to harm you, plans to give you hope and a future. Then you will call upon Me and come and pray to Me, and I will listen to you." (Jeremiah 29:11-12, NIV)

KICKING (CIGARETTE) BUTTS

As human beings, we manage to do quite a bit of damage without any help from our friends. For instance, choices we make as teenagers can sometimes affect our lives for many, many years, and when we make the initial decision, we usually don't even realize just how far-reaching that decision may extend. Decisions such as taking that first drink when our parents are gone; "only exhaling" that first joint; or going all the way to prove you "love that guy and just can't live without him" are only a few of the biggies. We rationalize with the best of them, too. The 90's culture used the excuse that there was no right or wrong, as long as nobody got hurt; the 80's used the excuse, "If it makes you feel good, do it!"; the 70's didn't need an excuse - it was the decade of ME; the growing up excuse is, "Everybody else is doing it," and then the time-honored excuse, "The devil made me do it."

So, once you've proven yourself to whomever it is you're proving yourself, then what? What happens when you "grow up" and find your choice is haunting you for whatever reason, whether mental, physical or spiritual? Well, just go figure this one out – there's Hope, and it's hope with a capital H!

JB

****

Judith Burhans

I never thought I'd actually be able to stop smoking, but I did – and all because I finally heard God knocking. Here's how it happened.

I was a smoker from age 17, and continuing through my college years, my marriage, two pregnancy-and-birth experiences, and on through my middle age. No, I'm not stupid, and yes, I did know how bad for me the cigarettes were—but addiction means you can't just snap your fingers and quit the filthy things.

At various points along the way, the clamor from health professionals, the media, my family and friends would get through to me; I would admit that the smoking was probably going to kill me; and I would launch yet another effort to quit. I tried cold turkey several times (lasting from an hour to almost a day), the nicotine gum (nasty!), and even hypnotism (I spent the session snickering about how bad the hypnotist was). I even tried the nicotine patches, but gave up on those when I realized I was smoking at the same time I was wearing the patch!

But most of the time I managed to ignore those voices telling me to quit. I came up with all kinds of rationalizations for why I should just keep smoking—things like

- Well, I smoke so much (2-3 packs per day) that the shock of quitting would probably be too much for my system.

- I'm already 30 pounds overweight, and if I quit I'll gain even more weight, and that would probably be worse for my heart than the actual smoking.

- It's probably healthy that I cough a lot and blow my nose a lot because that gets rid of all kinds of germs that might otherwise take up residence in my body.

- The cigarette industry is so large and so many people smoke, it can't be as bad for you as some people say. The world is always full of fanatics, and that's what the stop-smoking people are.

Then late in July of 1997, the doctor announced that he saw some "questionable areas" on my mammogram film, and he sent me to a surgeon for a biopsy. The surgeon explained how he would perform the biopsy, and we talked about how we would proceed if the biopsy indicated further surgery was needed. He was tossing around words like "lumpectomy" and "mastectomy" and "reconstructive surgery." Scared? Who me?! And during our talk, the surgeon said, "You know, this may turn out to be nothing, and if that's true, you will have dodged the bullet—this time. But your smoking is going to get you."

For some reason, that statement and all the other things in this conversation finally got to me, and I decided that yes, I had to quit. I bought another box of the nicotine patches, and the next morning (August 1, 1997) after smoking one last cigarette, I showered, shampooed, and got dressed. Then I stood in the middle of my bedroom with that first nicotine patch in my hand and did the most significant thing I'd ever done about stopping smoking: I asked the Lord to help me. "Please, God," I said, "You know I can't do this by myself. Could you help me?"

Did He answer me? YES! I made it through that day and the next without a cigarette! The next day was Sunday, and (still smoke-free) at church I went forward to kneel for communion. "Lord, thank you for helping me. Please continue to help me. Please take the nicotine habit from me." AND HE DID! He even gave me a sign that I could relax in His care. As I prayed those words, a rush of air seemed to be drawn from deep inside me and out through my mouth and nose, and in that instant I knew that the need for tobacco was gone from me. The Lord had taken it from me, and I felt a great release. From that time, I have not smoked; in fact, I haven't even wanted to! Praise God!

Oh, yes—and the icing on the cake was that the biopsy showed no need for further concern. No cancer!

How did God get my attention this time? Through a very scary medical situation. He really does use every event in our lives to communicate with us, but communication is a two-way activity. We have to answer His Knock-Knock. We have to pay attention and then follow through.

Kay Bradburn

****

Psalm 20:1-9 (NIV) seems to fit this story in its entirety:

"May the LORD answer you when you are in distress;

may the name of the God of Jacob protect you.

May He send you help from the sanctuary

and grant you support from Zion.

May He remember all your sacrifices

and accept your burnt offerings.

Selah

May He give you the desire of your heart

and make all your plans succeed.

We will shout for joy when you are victorious

and will lift up our banners in the name of our God.

May the LORD grant all your requests.

Now I know that the LORD saves His anointed;

He answers him from His holy heaven

with the saving power of His right hand.

Some trust in chariots and some in horses,

but we trust in the name of the LORD our God.

They are brought to their knees and fall,

but we rise up and stand firm.

O LORD, save the king!

Answer us when we call!"

MEET BENJAMIN

Many times, we find that we have no other option to "fix" something except to pray. While that can seem like a cop-out – we'd really rather try to <u>do</u> it ourselves and use our own creative solutions to problem solve – we find that if we'd prayed in the first place, more than likely, we wouldn't have been where we were when we discovered we were running around in circles! Never underestimate the power of prayer, especially when it comes from the bottom of your soul! And never think, for even a second, that God doesn't want to hear from you – for whatever reason – because He says He's ready to share everything with us, from the mundane to the monstrosities. So hey, why not? Give Him the worst you've got, and just see if He doesn't turn it all into praises and blessings!

JB

****

There are many characters in this story but the main one is Jesus and His power. I was a part of this story but I was also a witness to all of it and I'll never forget it.

This story is about my grandson, Benjamin. The beginning to Benjamin's life was rocky. He had inhaled amniotic fluid with feces during his birth and went into immediate pneumonia. He struggled very hard to live for the first few days in an Army hospital and was finally sent by helicopter to another hospital. He began to get better, but then started projectile vomiting with every feeding. He was diagnosed with pyloric stenosis and went into major surgery the same day.

I saw Benjamin for the first time when he was about 2 ½ weeks old. He had been released from the hospital only a few days. My daughter, Susie (the youngest of my three children), was struggling to cope with taking care of this little boy. He didn't cry – didn't want to eat – did not respond to her. I wondered if there were brain damage from the initial pneumonia and the days in the oxygen tent. I went home and prayed and prayed and prayed. Benjamin had been on every prayer line I could find since he was born.

The next time I saw Benjamin was about three weeks later. He was a different child – he was now eating well and smiling. He had a joy that was contagious and as he grew over the next few years he shared this joy with

the man she had married was someone else altogether. He was with her as she wept, screamed, slept and tried to get through each day.

Our lives changed. We needed a bigger place to live. Susie had to get a job. Benjamin had to go to day care in addition to pre-kindergarten. There are no words to describe his fear during that time. He would begin to cry the minute he woke up – not rebellious – just tears running down his cheeks. "Mom, please don't take me to school," "Mom, please stay at school with me," "Nannie, what time are you picking me up?" "Is it the weekend yet?" Over and over, he voiced his distress. Day after day, we watched this little boy cry. His joy was gone, as was ours.

Benjamin was in a Christian environment because the school and day care were part of my church. The teachers suggested counseling for him since he didn't play, didn't eat, and was always watching the door for his mother or me to return for him. He disrupted the class with his wailing, at times. Counseling was unproductive; how do you counsel a four-year-old? We tried everything we knew to comfort this child, but nothing helped. When would the school call us to say they just couldn't do it – that we would have to find another place for him?

All of this went on for about six weeks with absolutely no change. There are no words to tell you what it was like to live with this little boy who was so sad. Then one Wednesday evening, I went to direct my junior bell choir.

When I asked if anyone had a prayer request, a little girl named Anna said, "Let's pray for Benjamin."

I looked at her and said, "What would you like to pray for Benjamin?"

She said, "He's nervous – let's ask God to be with him and take away his fear."

Immediately all of the other children chimed in, agreeing with this, and we prayed for Benjamin.

Later that evening, Benjamin came into my room and said, "Nannie, you can talk about school now." The next morning, he said, "Nannie, you can talk about your work now and about mom's work – you can talk about ANYTHING!" This was said with his arms outstretched and a smile on his face.

Benjamin's wailing stopped. His fear left, he made friends, his smile was back in place and his joy returned - all on that day. We have thanked Jesus over and over and over. We thanked God for the children who cared enough for Benjamin to pray for him. We thanked God for all of the people who supported Benjamin and us through this time of trouble.

What will life bring for him and for us? I don't know this answer, but I know that God does listen to us and that He will be with us in all circumstances.

Susan Sadler

The Knock-Knock Book
If I Hear God Knocking, Do You Think I Should Answer?

****

"Therefore let everyone who is godly pray to You while You may be found; surely when the mighty waters rise, they will not reach Him. You are my hiding place; You will protect me from trouble and surround me with songs of deliverance." (Psalm 32:6-7, NIV)

Judith Burhans

For every situation in life, there is a Bible passage. Ecclesiastes 3:1-2, 6 fits perfectly with the following story: "There is a time for everything, and a season for every activity under heaven: a time to be born, a time to die...a time to search, a time to give up...

****

...A TIME TO MOVE, A TIME TO STAY PUT...

After living in a neighborhood in town for all 32 years of our married lives, my husband Charlie and I decided it was time to move to the country. We dreamed of leaving behind our older, two-story house and building or buying a house all on one level, a house with large, sunny rooms and as much land around it as we could afford—the more the better.

And so we started our search. Quickly, we chose the area of the county we liked best and discovered that the more conveniently close to town a piece of land was, the higher its price would be. In order to afford more than an acre or two, we would have to endure a fairly long commute to work. Since both of us would be retiring from our jobs in just a few more years, the commute to work became less of a consideration than the commute to our church, where we were deeply involved.

The search went on and on…and on. Most weekends, we spent at least an afternoon searching country lanes that looked promising, and every Sunday I would study the newspaper's "House for Sale" ads. Once each month, local realtors published several glossy magazines featuring properties for sale, and we became faithful readers of those. I made countless calls to realtors, following up leads, and I kept copious notes on the properties we inquired about and/or went to see.

We found charming houses on tiny lots; lovely pieces of land with horrible houses on them; great land with the perfect house that was so costly we could only laugh; great land with a suitable house but so far out of town, we'd have to give up sleep altogether to make time for the commute to work. Unfortunately, we could not find a place that felt right.

So, we decided to find a piece of land and build our own house. After another long search, we finally found a lovely piece of land in the right location, but it wasn't for sale. It was farmland and no one lived there, but an afternoon spent in the county courthouse records room revealed the owner's name—someone who didn't even live in our state. Inquiries among our friends turned up someone who knew how to contact the owner, and a long distance call finally reached her.

"Yes!" she said. She would consider selling us some of her acreage. It was land her husband and she had retired on, but he had died a year before, and she had moved to another state to be near her family. But she asked us to wait six months; Congress was expected to pass capital gains tax legislation that would enable her to sell. Happy to have found the perfect spot, we were content to wait. Meanwhile, we searched book after book, looking for the perfect house plan.

Months passed, house plan books stacked higher and higher, but we found no perfect house plan. Finally, I decided to draw one — me, the person who can't draw a straight line with a ruler! I would spend days laboring over my latest creation, but with each drawing, Charlie would damn it with faint praise: "Uh-huh, that's nice. Looks expensive to build, though," or "You really like that one, huh? Yeah, nice." But then, what was the hurry...Congress hadn't yet passed the tax legislation.

Then finally, in October, the law was passed! Quickly I phoned the landowner, but she asked me to phone one of her sons who lived in another town. She said there had been "sickness in the family."

Imagine my disappointment when the son informed me that the "sickness in the family" was, in fact, his mother. She'd been diagnosed with liver cancer and given a very brief time to live. He made it clear that the family didn't want to discuss selling any land then or any time in the foreseeable future, and of course, we understood.

And so our search began again, but hard as we tried, we still found neither house nor land.

Then, Knock-Knock…it finally occurred to me one day that maybe God didn't want us to move. You know, honestly, until that day, in spite of the fact that I am a Christian who prays daily and believes firmly that God loves and directs us — in spite of that, I hadn't invited God into this house and land search. But finally that day, I heard Him knocking, and so I prayed, "Lord, do you want us to move? Or do you want us to stay put? Whatever it is that you would have us do, would you please show us what that is?"

Well, my friend, God answered, and quickly! Apparently, He was just waiting to be asked into this situation, because within two weeks He had led us to the perfect house on the perfect ten acres of land in the perfect location! And within three weeks, we had bought it!

Judith Burhans

I "found" the house on the Internet, late one Sunday night; Monday morning we called the realtor and Monday afternoon we first visited the house. Both of us knew immediately that this was our house. In fact, I didn't want to leave! Laughing, I said to Charlie, "I'll lie down here; you go home and get our stuff!"

On Wednesday we made an offer, and by Saturday, after some back and forth, the seller had accepted our bid. Within weeks, we would be moving in!

But now I started to worry about all the work facing us, especially the part about fixing up our old house to make it sale-able and keeping up the yard work there while also maintaining our new place. The house next door to ours had taken a year to sell. Other houses in the neighborhood had taken a similar amount of time. "Lord," I prayed, "please help. I worry that Charlie will do too much."

And would you believe, that very week a friend who had heard the news of our impending move called to ask if we'd be selling our old house. It seems his son was looking for a house, and he wanted one in our neighborhood since it was convenient to his work. The very next day, Kevin came to see our house. Essentially, he said, "I want it. How much?" It turned out that Kevin preferred doing his own painting and fixing up, so we didn't even have to worry about that. Oh, yes! God IS good! And all I had to do was answer His Knock-Knock.

Kay Bradburn

****

"Therefore I tell you, do not worry about your life, what you will eat or drink; or about your body, what you will wear. Is not life more important than food, and the body more important than clothes? Look at the birds of the air; they do not sow or reap or store away in barns, and yet your heavenly Father feeds them. Are you not much more valuable than they? Who of you by worrying can add a single hour to his life?...So do not worry, saying, 'What shall we eat?' or 'What shall we drink?' or 'What shall we wear?' For the pagans run after all these things, and your heavenly Father knows that you need them. But seek first His kingdom and His righteousness, and all these things will be given to you as well. Therefore do not worry about tomorrow, for tomorrow will worry about itself. Each day has enough trouble of its own.

(Matthew 6:25-27; 31-34, NIV)

Judith Burhans

SAY WHAT?

The Old Testament is filled with stories about God speaking directly to people. But does He still do that? Have you ever heard Him speak? I mean, speak not through a song or a friend or a sermon or a Bible passage - but actually speak! A friend of ours tells the following story about just such an experience.

JB

****

Grace and William have been happily married for many years, and this story took place about eight or nine years into their marriage. Grace has always been extremely active at church - regular in attendance, a member of the choir, etc. - but William's church activity was limited strictly to attending 11:00 worship service. He never objected to going to church, but the second the service ended, he was out the door, into the car, and on the road for home. And he never wanted to attend church suppers or any of the other parish activities.

Grace and William had two young children, a daughter 7 years old at the time of this story and a son, then 2. Grace was determined to bring up her children in the church, and while William didn't object, he didn't do much to help. For one thing, he wouldn't go to Sunday School. Sometimes Grace would take the children by herself and William would drive to church separately, when it was time for worship service. Other times the family would arrive together at the Sunday School hour, but William would wait in the car until time for worship service to begin.

Daughter Angie would ask, "Mommy, why is Daddy sitting in the car?" Or son Will, Jr. would demand, "Play with Daddy in the car!" When an activity like the church picnic was announced, Angie would beg, "Oh, can we go, Mommy? Can we go?"

Week after week, Grace found herself making excuses for William: "Daddy doesn't feel good right now. Let's let him rest." Or, "Sorry, honey. Maybe next time there's a dinner..."

Grace prayed every day that God would change William's heart, that He would send someone to say just the right words so that William's cold shoulder toward church activities would thaw. William's reluctance to participate, Grace knew, stemmed from an experience he'd gone through as a teenager. The young people at his church, inspired by a fiery evangelist, had made a spectacle of themselves at school, falling to their knees right there in the school cafeteria and praying for people to be "saved" who were already firm believers in God. William, embarrassed by his peers, had retreated from that group of gung ho youth and from any church activity that might require him to open his heart.

But as each week brought more questions from the children, Grace's worry level increased. She worried that if she cornered William about the matter, he would just quit going to church completely. She also worried that if things didn't change, the children would adopt William's attitude.

Then one day, a Saturday morning, Grace arrived early for a meeting at the church and found no one there except the pastor, who was busy in his office. Grace wandered into the sanctuary and sat down two rows back from the altar. The stained glass windows let in just enough light to give the room a comfortable, twilight feel, and Grace bowed her head, once again to plead with God to solve her dilemma.

"Please, Lord, send someone to speak to William about his attitude. Please, Lord."

Grace says, "And that's when it happened…I heard His voice! I mean I didn't hear it, hear it, like in a sound that was outside my head but in the room with me. It was more like I heard Him speak inside my mind. But I was absolutely sure that it was His voice. And God said these words to me: 'You do it.'"

"That's it...just those three words. I was thunderstruck!" Grace says.

"It just took my breath away, and I sat there with my mouth literally hanging open. God Himself had spoken to me!"

"I sat there another half hour or so, gradually getting more accustomed to the idea that God had spoken directly to me, and gradually realized that He wasn't going to go into detail. He'd said 'You do it,' and then He'd left it up to me how to carry this out...or whether to carry it out."

"All that day, I worried about whether to bring up the subject with William, and if I did bring it up, what to say. Finally, it was bedtime. As I climbed into bed beside my husband, I said, 'William, tomorrow morning I'm going to take the kids to Sunday School, and I'm going to Sunday School, too. I hope you'll come with us, but if you don't, I'm not going to alibi for you. If the kids want to know why you don't go to Sunday School too, I'm going to tell them to ask you.' Then I held my breath and waited to see how he would react."

Several minutes passed and he didn't say anything. Then his only response was a matter of fact, "Okay." I had no idea what that meant, but I fully intended to do just what I'd said.

Grace went on to say that the next morning, she dressed herself and the children in their Sunday clothes, and William got his good clothes on too! The whole family got into the car, and William drove them to the church. Then, the entire family - including William - attended Sunday School! At the end of the worship service that morning, the pastor reminded the congregation of a covered dish dinner that would take place that evening.

As the family strolled down the sidewalk to their car, William asked his family, "Shall we come to the dinner tonight?"

"YES, YES, YES!" chimed a delighted Angie and Will, dancing up and down.

That was many years ago, says Grace, and from that day to this, her William has been willing to do far more than just attend 11:00 worship service. All because of one little sentence God spoke to the heart of a worried mother and wife…and because that wife and mother was listening and was willing to act on God's word.

Author Anonymous

"Ask and it will be given to you; seek and you will find; knock and the door will be opened to you. For everyone who asks receives; he who seeks finds; and to him who knocks, the door will be opened." (Matthew 7:7 NIV)

Judith Burhans

PART IV
POSITION NEEDED: MOM

JOB DESCRIPTION: Long term team players needed for challenging permanent work in an often-chaotic environment. Candidates must possess excellent communication and organizational skills and be willing to work variable hours, which will include evenings and weekends and frequent 24-hour shifts on call. Some overnight travel required, including trips to primitive camping sites on rainy weekends and endless sports tournaments in faraway cities. Travel expenses not reimbursed. Extensive courier duties also required.

RESPONSIBILITIES: Must provide on-the-site training in basic life skills, such as nose blowing. Must have strong skills in negotiating, conflict resolution and crisis management. Ability to suture flesh wounds a plus. Must be able to think out of the box, but not lose track of the box, because you most likely will need it for a school project. Must reconcile petty cash disbursements and be proficient in managing budgets and resources fairly, unless you want to hear, "He got more than me!" for the rest of your life. Also, must be able to drive motor vehicles safely under loud and adverse conditions while simultaneously practicing above-mentioned skills in conflict resolution. Must be able to choose your battles and stick to your guns. Must be able to withstand criticism, such as "You don't know anything." Must be willing to be hated at least temporarily, until someone needs $5 to go skating. Must be willing to bite tongue repeatedly. Also, must possess the physical stamina of a pack mule and be able to go from zero to 60 mph in three seconds flat in case, this time, the screams from the backyard are not someone just crying wolf. Must be willing to face stimulating technical challenges, such as small gadget repair, mysteriously sluggish toilets and stuck zippers. Must screen phone calls, maintain calendars and coordinate production of multiple homework projects. Must have ability to plan and organize social gatherings for clients of all ages and mental outlooks. Must be willing to be indispensable one minute, an embarrassment the next. Must handle assembly and product safety testing of a half million cheap, plastic toys and battery operated devices. Also, must have a highly energetic entrepreneurial spirit, because fund-raiser will be your middle name. Must have a diverse knowledge base, so as to answer questions such as "What makes the wind move?" on the fly. Must always hope for the best but be prepared for the worst. Must assume final, complete accountability for the quality of the end product. Responsibilities also include floor maintenance and janitorial work throughout the facility.

POSSIBILITY FOR ADVANCEMENT AND PROMOTION: Virtually none. Your job is to remain in the same position for years, without complaining, constantly retraining and updating your skills, so that those in your charge can ultimately surpass you.

PREVIOUS EXPERIENCE: None required, unfortunately. On-the-job training offered on a continually exhausting basis.

WAGES AND COMPENSATION: You pay them, offering frequent raises and bonuses. A balloon payment is due when they turn 18 because of the assumption that college will help them become financially independent. When you die, you give them whatever is left. The oddest thing about this reverse-salary scheme is that you actually enjoy it and wish you could only do more.

BENEFITS: While no health or dental insurance, no pension, no tuition reimbursement, no paid holidays and no stock options are offered, job supplies limitless opportunities for personal growth and free hugs for life if you play your cards right.

Internet

****

HOW TO BECOME A MOM WITHOUT REALLY TRYING

(OR, UNEXPECTED GIFTS)

Becoming a mom is like being a child – there are no directions that come with the position. God willing, however, most of us make it through the process – somehow – and live to tell about it. There have been a lot of books written on child rearing and child discipline and child-this and child-that, none of which I've read thoroughly, mainly because I don't like to compare myself to "perfect" parents with "perfect" kids. My best clue for raising kids, and the only advice I could possibly give for raising kids, would be to love that child where he is, for what he is, for who he is, and to give that love unconditionally. And most important, PRAY UNCEASINGLY, for that child and for YOURSELF!

JB

****

Kids – I have kids. I have all kinds of kids and most of them are not even mine. In fact, some of the kids don't even know whose they are, so I guess we're pretty even. How does life get so complicated?

Judith Burhans

Welcome to the home of a foster family. Lots of people seem to think we, as a family, are many different adjectives as a family — wonderful, kind, good people, patient, NUTS — but let me tell you, we're none of the above (well, probably we're nuts). Let me explain...

It all started one year when I was working at a hospital in Labor and Delivery, and just before I got off a 12-hour shift, a baby was brought into the emergency room downstairs. The child had been born at home, unknown to the grandparents who were living in the same home. The mother had stabbed the child many, many times in the neck and throat area, then shoved the baby under the bed, thinking he was dead. She woke up her parents to tell them she was bleeding and needed to go to the hospital. The baby's grandmother brought "mom" to the hospital, and in the meantime, grandfather heard a sound coming from his daughter's room and went to investigate. He's the one who found the baby, still alive, and brought the child to the same emergency room where his daughter was being treated.

Sad story, isn't it? Did I hear a knock-knock all the way home that morning? Boy, did I!

Since that day, we have been dealing with foster children and the government-sanctioned Department of Human Resources (DHR) for many,

many years. We have had children in our home who started out not being ours, but who have ended up being ours, either through adoption or VERY long-term foster care. We've only had four children in 15 years who have actually left our care before they, or we, were ready. One ran away so she could marry some guy whose name she didn't even know; one was placed with his sibling in another foster home; Bradley, our very first foster child who "broke us in"; and Matthew James, the really special little guy of my life.

When we first started our "career" in foster care, we were given a tiny baby who we were told would only be in our home for three months or less. Point 1: When you start working with DHR in our state, you find out, really quickly, that "three months" doesn't mean three months; "until the next court hearing in September" doesn't necessarily mean the next court hearing in September <u>of this year</u>; and, "we only need you to keep her/him over the weekend until we can find another place" doesn't mean anything at all. That "over the weekend," in our case, was 3-1/2 years ago and the children are still here! Anyway, I digress.

The first baby, as I said, came to our house, only three weeks old. Naturally, we all fell in love with him on sight. Three months turned into 10 months, at which time we had our first heartbreak — we had to give him back so his great-aunt could adopt him. At that time, our state would not let foster parents adopt the children they were fostering. That has since changed, although at that time, that was the rule, and we had to give up this baby. He was just starting to walk and was the center of our attention. I told my family (and they told me) that we were through with foster care – we weren't taking any more kids because we were all crying, all the time, any time we thought about Bradley or anyone mentioned his name. That was that.

Two months later, a social worker from a different county called and said, "I'm Miss Whoever from outside of your county, and I know you have not specified that you'll care for foster children with special needs, but your department told me that you might consider taking this baby…" She went on to tell me all about Baby Boy Smith, whose mother had put him up for adoption before he was even born, and who had adoptive parents all lined up. When this baby was born with severe brain damage (hydranencephaly), the prospective adoptive parents didn't want him, and the mother left the hospital without naming him. At the time the social worker called us, he was then five weeks old, his condition was "stable," and the hospital staff had to discharge him that week. Supposedly, this social worker had called all the foster parents in her county and had gotten no takers, and she had called us as the last resort – If we didn't want him, he would go to a nursing home. The doctors only gave him one year to live with his diagnosis. If we didn't take him, he would at least have daily nursing care – in a nursing home.

Well, well, well. Let me think about this. A baby who has brain damage to the extent that he only has a brain stem. He has no bodily temperature control because his brain didn't form a thermostat; he has no vision (according to the doctors) because his brain didn't form optic nerves that worked; he can't hear (also according to the doctors). He would never grow up because his lungs wouldn't support his body that long; we'd only have to keep him about a year because the doctors said that's the maximum amount of time children like this live; and nobody would come and take him away from us because nobody wanted him. He sounded like a keeper to me!

I said, "Yes, we'll take him. When can you bring him here, or do we have to come get him?"

She said, "Are you sure? Don't you need to talk this over with your husband?"

I said, "Yes...No...When can we get him?"

Three days later, life with Matthew James began. Now, remember, he was still legally named "Baby Boy Smith," but we're from up north where every family I've ever known has children with NAMES, so we gave him a name, even if it wasn't legal. Matthew James weighed a grand total of seven pounds, and I think all but two of those pounds were in his head. He had only a brainstem, so he could cry, eat, sleep and had basic reflexes, but he also had the hydrocephalus, the extra fluid in the brain cavity, so he had a shunt already placed in his head that drained into his abdomen. He was a skinny little guy, and all of his baby hair had been shaved off because of the shunt surgery, but he was the most beautiful baby I had seen since my own children had been born. He was also asleep, at that point.

Point II: Social workers are known for telling you just enough to give you a clue as to what to expect – maybe – but then, they don't spend enough time with any of these children to really KNOW what to expect, themselves, so everybody gets surprises. In Matthew's case, it was that when he was awake, he cried constantly, no matter what anyone did with him. He refused pacifiers of ANY shape, he refused to fall asleep like a normal child while drinking a bottle. He had a high-pitched cry because of his brain damage, and this quickly became music to no one's ears! The most embarrassing moment for me, with Matthew crying constantly, came in the commissary where I was shopping for groceries. He was crying and crying and crying, and naturally, you pass and re-pass so many people down the aisles as you shop. This one woman, in particular, seemed to scowl at me every time we passed, because I couldn't seem to take care of this child. On the fourth pass, I just ignored her, since I really had nothing to tell her, and I figured it wasn't her business if Matthew cried just to hear himself emote, anyway!

Finally, four months after we got him, my sister-in-law and I were at my parents' house at the same time. Up north, there is a liquid children's aspirin known as Liquiprin, and it comes in a bottle with a stopper on it to measure out dosages. Pam said, "Why don't you try putting the stopper in Matthew's mouth and see what happens?" Well, God bless Pam! Matthew was able to feel the end of the stopper on the roof of his mouth, something he couldn't do with any of the other pacifiers, I guess, and a miracle occurred - he quit crying! Just to make sure it wasn't a fluke, I pulled the stopper out of his mouth, and he started crying, again. Put the stopper back in, quiet. It was wonderful! Not only did we have a new pacifier, but we had liquid aspirin that we could also use for him if we thought he might be feeling bad. (It's hard to tell if a child has a fever if the child doesn't even have a temperature regulator in the first place. Think about that!)

Judith Burhans

From that point on, life with a "normal" Matthew began - normal being defined as having some sort of control over his crying, most of the time. Our schedule that first year looked something like this:

- October – Matthew delivered to our house.
- November (Thanksgiving, to be exact) – Shunt blocked, trip to Children's Hospital for surgery.
- December (Christmas) – Shunt blocked, trip south on the interstate to the Children's Hospital rather than north on the interstate to Indiana to see family; presents in the trunk replaced with suitcase for Matthew and me for however long a stay in the hospital.
- February (Valentine's Day) – overnight stay at local hospital for rehydration. Any typical, "common" cold for a typical, "common" child had dire effects on Matthew because his little body had a "not great" immune system with which to fight diseases.
- April (Easter) – Trip to Children's Hospital for another shunt revision. Do you see Matthew's plan to spend holidays in hospitals??
- July 4th weekend – Shunt revision.
- Thanksgiving – Back to try the turkey, again, and another shunt revision.

- December 19 – January 3 – This was a scary stay.

Matthew now weighed 12 whole pounds, and his shunt blocked up, again. Naturally, it was a big holiday, the second Christmas in a row we were going to miss going up north, again. Not a single child in the house complained, not a single relative ranted or raved. The social worker told me I didn't have to stay in the hospital with him, since I was <u>only</u> his foster mother, and I told her that's why I was staying, because I <u>was</u> his foster mother. I had just found out I was pregnant with my third child. My husband, who was in the Army, had orders to be out in Kansas January 1, and our house had a closing date for selling it right after Christmas. I still had two other children, but since we were soon to be homeless, they got to head north to stay with their grandparents, thanks to an acquaintance who was going that way, and Steven and I stayed in the south. He got to finish cleaning the house for the sale, I stayed with Matthew in the hospital.

This hospital admission was similar to others, initially. Matthew had the fontanelle that was bulging, surgery was scheduled for the next day, and surgery progressed, as usual. The resident took out the old shunt and replaced it with a new shunt, closed Matthew's head with stitches, and then cultured the fluid from the old shunt. It was from that point that everything that could, did, go wrong. The fluid was full of bacteria, and when the resident had removed the old shunt, the fluid that drained into Matthew caused a sepsis throughout his whole body. This meant that the following day, Matthew had a second surgery to take out the "new" shunt, replace it with an external system for drainage (ventriculostomy), but until the body cleared the sepsis, he could not have the internal shunt put back in. This meant that with the ventriculostomy, the tube drained from his head <u>out</u> to a collecting bag, and Matthew had to stay inclined at a certain angle when the tubing was open so the fluid could drain, yet keep an equilibrium with the brain. He had to stay in this position all the time, and if I were to hold him, I had to clamp off the tubing so that no drainage occurred. I could only hold him for a maximum of 20 minutes at a time; otherwise, the pressure in his head would increase to the point that seizures could occur.

Matthew spent the next 10 days fighting for his life. His weight went from 12 pounds to 19 pounds, but the extra seven pounds weren't "good" pounds – they were pounds of infected fluid, causing swelling in his body. Antibiotics were administered daily through the ventriculostomy in his head. Blood was drawn all the time, and if you can imagine, Matthew's circulatory system was never very good, even when he was at his best. When he was sick and dehydrated, his veins were practically impossible to get a catheter into for blood. When I got comfortable being in the hospital setting as a parent, I began to ask for only the best "blood-stickers" they had, because anyone less would blow the few 'possible' veins he had. Then they'd try a cut-down – literally cutting into his ankles to split open a vein into which they could try to insert a catheter for both a blood draw and a subsequent IV. The one time they tried this on him, they were unable to get the blood they needed, and after that experience, I refused any more cut-downs on him.

Matthew's arms eventually became little purple pincushions. A couple of mornings when he was so sick, I thought he wouldn't make it - he didn't even flinch when the lab people came for his morning draw. He didn't open his eyes, he didn't move, he didn't cry, he didn't whimper. That was my darkest point of that hospitalization, and I could only cry and cry.

There were many times during that hospital stay I just knew that if Matthew had not been a Medicaid child, just another number, he would not have been in that position. Shouldn't the resident have checked the shunt fluid before he took out the shunt and inserted a new one? Would that have stopped the spread of the bacteria through this little boy's compromised body? Even the doctor in charge of the case came into the room during one of those 10 bug-fighting days and said, "Well, you know, he's living on borrowed time as it is, and you're lucky you've kept him alive as long as you have."

I learned quite a few things during that hospital stay, and during the whole time Matthew was with us, but these were the two biggest lessons learned: (1) how to bite my tongue - probably the biggest lesson; and (2) why God put Matthew into my life. It wasn't because Matthew needed me and what I could do for him with my gifts, but rather, I needed Matthew! He taught me, and our whole family, that life was a precious gift and one over which, ultimately, we have absolutely no control. So quickly, life as we know it can be gone, and not just by death or dying.

When we have our health, we function daily as God made us to function, and we may not even realize some people have to live with much less – unless we deal with those special people. Well, we "realize" it, but I don't think it affects us unless we deal with it personally and close to home. Matthew taught me that in his condition of not being able to tell us what was wrong, what he needed, or what was hurting, he had to rely on us to KNOW - and to provide. Wow! What if we weren't paying attention?

Matthew could hear – the doctors were wrong about that. His little eyes would move around to where he heard a sound or a voice, and he'd try to "see" us; he would be comforted with our voices, most of the time. He would also stop crying, sometimes, if a light were turned on at night, so he must have had some sort of sense of light and dark.

Matthew could love. Oh, he could love! He gave his little heart to anybody who needed it. He could smile and he could laugh – a deep chuckle that came from such a small body, or a funny giggle if we could find his "tickle" spot, which we could. He could lie across my lap or shoulders for hours at a time and be satisfied. Matthew and I stretched out on the sofa many, many summers and "watched" the Braves and Cubs baseball games. I'd tell Steven that Matthew and I were going to watch the ball game and he'd have to do the dishes, and for 10 summers, it worked! Whatever Matthew got out of those days and nights snuggling for warmth and comfort, I got so much more.

Nicholas, my one son, would pick up Matthew (also my son, since we did adopt him and give him a legal name!) from the Learning Development Center for special needs children, put one of his caps on Matthew with the bill in the back, perch a pair of sunglasses on his face, and they'd go four-wheeling before coming home. Matthew would be laughing when Nicholas finally brought him home. Nicholas would hold Matthew up to his face and say, "We're twins, can you tell?" or, "Which one's the big brother?"

Before Nicholas went away to basic training in February, he and Matthew had their pictures taken at an Olan Mills studio, and in the picture, they were both smiling so big, they did look like brothers. Nicholas said the photographer asked him what he was doing to make the baby laugh, and Nicholas swore he wasn't doing anything, other than holding him. Matthew had joy! Then, when Nicholas went away to basic training in February, Matthew's laugh was not heard again until we went to visit Nicholas during Easter at his training camp. As soon as Nicholas got into the van and said, "Hi, guys!" Matthew laughed! We knew then, for sure, who held Matthew's heart in our family!

Our days and time with Matthew were numbered; we all knew it, but we tried not to dwell on it. Matthew was heading into the two-digit mark in age – quite a few more years than the doctors predicted - and every year we could say, "Thank you, God, for Matthew, and for the doctors not knowing everything!"

Winter was always the worst time for Matthew, and pneumonia was the culprit that we hoped would never happen. Pneumonia never did, but Matthew's little body had finally had enough, and God decided He wanted Matthew's smile close to Him. In the middle of January, Matthew woke me up around 4:30 AM, fussed and fussed until I turned his head and repositioned him so he could go back to sleep, and that was all he wanted. I remember saying, "Well, Matthew, if you wanted me to do something, why didn't you just say something?" Of course, he had said something, the best way he knew how. That was our good-bye. I woke up two hours later, and Matthew had already gone home with his best friend, Jesus.

Judy Burhans

****

"But now, this is what the LORD says— He *who created you,* O Jacob (and Matthew!), He *who formed you,* O Israel: 'Fear not, for I have redeemed you; I have summoned you by name; <u>you are Mine</u>.'" (Isaiah 43:1 NIV)

Judith Burhans

JOSH'S GRASP

A mother's love doesn't start after a child is born; it doesn't even start WHEN the child is born. If you were to ask a woman when she started loving her baby, if she gave the question enough thought, I bet she would have to say, "It began before I even had this child." Women spend nine months — sometimes nine LONG months, but nine months, nevertheless — in production, and while many changes are happening to the outsides of their bodies, something is happening inside to their hearts and their minds. I think that nine-month incubation period is good for more than just growing a baby; it's also a good time for a bond that starts to form and only gets stronger and stronger as time goes on.

JB

****

Our son Joshua was rambunctious in the womb, and arrived in this world eager to reach out and grasp life. When he was first handed to me, wrapped snugly in a blanket, just minutes after his birth, he lifted his head unlike a newborn, looked me in the face, and then worked his hand out of the blanket and grasped my fingers. He maintained a strong grip with three of his fingers wrapped around two of my fingers and then closed his eyes and went to sleep. I nursed that boy for nine months and he almost always fell asleep in my arms with his baby's grip strong around my fingers.

Our children grew up quickly as they all seem to do. In a flurry of Boy Scouts, parties, picnics, debate team, catechism classes, youth groups, Young Life, dances, banquets, and soccer, we participated in each step of the growth process. "These are the best years of your life," my mother would say every time I moaned about how busy we were. "Enjoy them because soon they'll be gone," she always said.

Teenage years are difficult, at best, for the parents and for the soon-to-be-adults. Sometimes I had to agree with the old adage that a child should be buried up to the neck at 13 and fed and watered like a plant until you can uproot them at 21 after they have gained some sense. Josh was in high school before he started the silent treatments that his friends' mothers had been describing their sons having for years. Josh had always been open with everything—smiling and confiding all the juicy details—but all of a sudden, at age 16, we started getting mostly one-syllable responses that were difficult to understand.

"Did you have a good day?" I ask when he walks into the house.

"Um," he grunts.

"Are you hungry?" I ask, thinking he'll give me a big smile when he smells the sauce cooking on the stove.

"Um," he replies, heading to his room to change out of his soccer clothes.

"Are you going to the dance?" I venture to ask.

"Yeah," he responds.

"How's school going?" I question.

"Good," as he turns on the PlayStation.

I knew he loved me and I knew he was trying to grow up and handle things himself, but sometimes, I just wanted my baby back for awhile.

Then one Saturday morning during the spring of his junior year in high school, he awoke with his eyes glassy with a high fever. He took some Tylenol and went back to bed. I checked on him later and he was in a bundle under the covers, sweating profusely.

"Mom I'm so sick," he murmured.

"I know, honey, I know," I whispered to my boy. "Here, get under this dry blanket, son. Turn over and I'll rub your back for you."

He turned over and I rubbed his back as I prayed. "Dear Lord, thank you for my son. Please watch over him during this sickness. Please bring his fever down so that he can get some sleep." I leaned over to brush his wet hair from his face and wrapped my arms around him the same as when he was a baby. As I kissed him on the forehead, I thought back to that first time he was put into my arms. And just at that moment, he pulled his right arm out of the cover and grasped two of my fingers with three of his fingers—the same baby's grip that he had used when falling asleep in my arms during the first nine months of his life.

I still cry whenever I sit and think about the miracle that God gave me that day. He made time stand still for over an hour as I was allowed to go back in time to smell my baby's hair, listen to his soft breathing sounds, and best of all, feel the strong grip of his three fingers wrapped around two of mine.

Sandy McCutcheon

****

"Listen, my son, accept what I say, and the years of your life will be many. I guide you in the way of wisdom and lead you along straight paths. When you walk, your steps will not be hampered; Hold on to instruction, do not let it go; guard it well, for it is your life." (Proverbs 4:10-13, NIV)

Judith Burhans

ABOVE AND BEYOND

Moms have to put up with the strangest things, sometimes, all in the name of motherhood. We become heroines and tyrants to our children at various points of their lives, and sometimes we're both, all in the same day! Could it be that God also likes the "knock-knock" jokes, and sometimes when we answer His knock, it's really for the comic relief of the day? What a great God!

JB

****

We were moving from Phoenix to Kansas City and I was at the end of my rope. Bob had already flown the coop to start his new job in KC, and I was left to sell the house (which means keeping it immaculate for incoming inspections from realtors/prospective buyers); deal with the packers/movers; and constantly reassure our children that this move was a very positive adventure. D'Arcy, age nine, and Josh, age four, were excited yet quite concerned about missing their friends, the school, and our house. I felt positive about the move, but my strength was dwindling by the hour. After almost a month without Bob there to share the stress and rub my back at night, I was being "stretched" to new dimensions. My daily/hourly/minute-by-minute prayers had gotten short and demanding, "Lord, get me with my husband."

The last day in our house included losing Chrissie, a cat that had been part of our family for five years, having to hire someone at the last minute to finish cleaning the laundry room/garage, checking the boxes, and working feverishly at a thousand other tasks. Finally, I found myself sliding down the wall with the phone in my hand, crying, "Bob, I just don't think I can make it to the hotel." He tried to keep me calm and kept saying, "Just one more day, honey. Tonight you stay in the hotel and tomorrow you get on the plane. Just one more day, honey."

D'Arcy cried constantly over losing Chrissie the cat and wouldn't let Sax, the four-year-old kitty (Chrissie's son) out of her arms. I knew the hotel wouldn't allow the cat, but finally, to prevent further trauma, I consented to sneak the cat into the hotel. Besides, I had paid $75 to have the cats checked out by our vet so they could travel and even had kitty tranquilizers for them. We may have been down a cat, but I wasn't about to be down two cats. I was going to make sure Sax stayed in his cage and in our eyesight that night.

Josh asked, "Does Jeepers have a cage? Will he be in with the cats?" Uh-oh! With all my planning and coordinating, I had not checked off one final mark on my list – how do you fly a green tree snake? Can cold-blooded reptiles survive in the baggage section of a plane like warm-blooded dogs and cats?

Now, for any of you who are wondering how in the world I could allow a snake in my house as a pet, let me tell you - this was the best pet we ever had. Very little cleanup was involved and the tiny snake ate crickets, occasionally – no litter box to clean, no astronomical food bills, and very little needed as far as vet bills. I had come to love this little no-teeth, no-maintenance green snake with the large black eyes. We had allowed the kids to name him (her?) and they had christened him (her?) "Jeepers, Creepers, Look at Those Peepers." We called him (her?) Jeepers for short.

I called the airline and no, they did not allow air travel for snakes. I went down the directory pages calling vets and animal retail stores and no, nobody had ever flown a snake. Well, I had reached my limit. The last shop was a large retail store, and I asked to speak with the owner. I told my story and said, "Look, I know you have snakes in that store. I know you have to purchase them elsewhere or travel with them occasionally. I'm at the end of my rope and you need to tell me how you get them from one city to another. I promise I will never release your name, but you have to tell me!"

I don't know if it had anything to do with his hearing the hysteria in my voice and thinking I might do him bodily harm, but the man said, "Okay, but you need to be very careful. You place the snake in a pillow slip and then tie it around your waist until you get on the plane. You then make sure the snake can breathe and place it in a large purse or bag for the remainder of the trip on the plane. You then do the same thing getting off the plane."

Oh, my goodness! Never in my wildest dreams did I imagine I was going to have to "wear" Jeepers to Kansas City! I took him in his cage to the hotel, sneaking him in with the cat, and stared at him all night. Finally, I decided that I didn't really have a problem "wearing" him as a belt in a pillowcase, especially after losing Chrissie the cat. I couldn't take one more bit of drama in my life so that was that, decision made. I packed an innocent-looking green and yellow floral pillowcase in the old brown Samsonite cosmetic case that was full of Legos, Barbies, crayons, and the various mix of toys and books one takes with kids on a trip.

Next morning at the airport, I said, "Okay, kids, into the bathroom," and I shepherded them into the ladies' room closest to our gate. The conspiracy was on! As a last reminder to Josh, I said, "Do not say 'Jeepers,' do not say 'snake,' do not ask if Jeepers can breathe okay, and do not ask anything about either my waist or the snake tied around my waist." Josh, with his big brown eyes very serious, said he understood. D'Arcy nodded her head and reached out to touch me as if to say, "It's all right, Mom." I went into the stall and did the deed – putting Jeepers into the pillowcase, tying him around my waist, and dropping the sweatshirt over my shorts.

We waited until almost time for the plane to take off to go through the x-ray machine, and it was then that the worst part of this nightmare began. The buzzer went off. The lady behind the machine looked at her TV screen and then intently at me; then she picked up her walkie-talkie and called for backup. Four uniformed officers approached us, extremely serious looks on their faces, and one of them kept his hand near his gun. The lady told us to stay where we were, and I nervously asked, "What's wrong?" Inside my screaming brain, I was thinking, "Oh, my goodness! They're going to search us! What kind of a nut will they think I am with a snake tied around my waist? I wonder if this if a felony?"

"What kind of a weapon is this?" the stern man asked, opening the cosmetic case and pulling out a very real-looking black toy gun. I laughed and said, "It's Josh's; it's a toy." But they weren't smiling. How was I to know you couldn't take a toy gun on an airplane?

Our flight was called for last boarding and I panicked again, thinking, "They aren't letting us go! They're going to search me! D'Arcy can keep her mouth shut, but a four-year-old boy can only go so long without asking about his snake tied around my waist. If we're in this much trouble for a toy-gun, what will they do when they find the snake?"

I think the lady officer must have been a mother, though, because when I started talking very fast, telling all about how we were moving and we had lost a family pet and I hadn't seen my husband in over a month and I had handled the entire move on my own and I just needed to get on that plane – I saw her eyes soften. I pounced on this opening and told the man who had Josh's toy gun in his hand that if he would look in the barrel, he could see not an orange bullet but a piece of orange crayon that had broken off in there. I said, "Keep the toy! Just please let me get on the plane!"

Peering into the barrel, he saw the crayon and said, "Okay, we'll let you go this time, but you need to realize you can never take toy guns on an airplane."

Judith Burhans

We left the gun, ran through the gate, and watched the door reopen to let us in the plane. Once at our seats, I quietly told Josh that I was going to the bathroom and with a big wink I said, "JEEPERS, Josh, you need to be really quiet on the airplane." He had flown enough to know that you don't have to be really quiet on an airplane so he caught my drift.

In the bathroom I removed the pillowcase/snake belt. Jeepers appeared to be asleep, but maybe I had stopped the flow of blood to his brain with the belt effect for so long. I opened the pillowcase and when he finally started to move, I tied a knot in the end and went back to our seats. Josh already had the cosmetic case out and was playing with the Legos, so I just tossed the pillowcase down under the seat in the middle. As the plane picked up speed, so did Jeepers, but by this time I didn't care. I was on the way to see my husband, to hand over all the responsibilities of children and pets, and I was going to get a back rub and a good night's sleep.

The rest of my trip to Kansas City that day was very peaceful. I wish I could say the same for the elderly gentleman who sat next to the window. He never said a word, but for the entire flight, he never took his eyes off the gently swaying green and yellow floral pillowcase. He had looked me in the face when I first sat down next to him, and he must have seen that wild look at least once in his own mother's eyes and figured it out. After all, what won't a mother do for her kids?

Sandy McCutcheon

****

"Your love, O LORD, reaches to the heavens,

Your faithfulness to the skies.

Your righteousness is like the mighty mountains,

Your justice like the great deep.

O LORD, You preserve both man and beast.

How priceless is Your unfailing love!" (Psalm 36:5-7, NIV)

Judith Burhans

PART V

THE MOM BEFORE ME

At some point in our lives, we realize we've finally grown up and our perspectives change — on a lot of things! Probably the most clear-cut indication of realizing just how much we really have grown up comes when we've done or said something, and then we stop and think, "Oh, no! I've turned into my mother!" Now, that might or might not be such a bad thing, but however it is for you, here's another offering from the Internet that, once again, sums up in a few words what our mothers might have meant to us.

THE IMAGES OF MOTHER

4 YEARS OF AGE	My Mommy can do anything!
8 YEARS OF AGE	My Mom knows a lot! A whole lot!
12 YEARS OF AGE	My Mother doesn't really know quite everything.
14 YEARS OF AGE	Naturally, Mother doesn't know that, either.
16 YEARS OF AGE	Mother? She's hopelessly old-fashioned.

The Knock-Knock Book
If I Hear God Knocking, Do You Think I Should Answer?

18 YEARS OF AGE	That old woman? She's way out of date!
25 YEARS OF AGE	Well, she might know a little bit about it.
35 YEARS OF AGE	Before we decide, let's get Mom's opinion.
45 YEARS OF AGE	Wonder what Mom would have thought about it?
65 YEARS OF AGE	Wish I could talk it over with Mom.

Internet

****

Judith Burhans

THE SPITTIN' IMAGE OF JEAN

The title of this story comes from a phrase I heard when I was visiting my grandmother up in Canada one year for the summer. I was out in her garden picking beans and eating fresh rhubarb (probably more the latter than the former), when I heard her tell some neighbor who had been walking by, "This is my granddaughter, Judy. Isn't she the spittin' image of Jean?" Well, I had no idea what my grandmother was talking about, but to use the word 'spit' in the same sentence as both my mother AND me, I didn't think it could mean anything good!

By the time the neighbor left and the chat session was over, I promptly went to find my grandmother and asked her just exactly what she meant by "spittin' image" of mom and me – and she told me. Unfortunately, her explanation that I was just like my mother didn't set too well with me, either. I mean, I was only about six or seven, and my mom was, well, my mom! She was a LOT older than I was, so how could I possibly be just like her? I saw absolutely no resemblance, at all.

Well, well, well – time marches on, doesn't it? I eventually came to understand what "spittin' image" meant, and I suppose I can see similarities, but it's more in the things she taught me to do rather than in the physical aspects that I can find the connection. Even temperamentally, we're different. She worries about everything; I don't have time to worry. She gives the "silent" treatment when she's upset or mad; I blow up – if I think it's worth blowing up over. She very seldom gives hugs for "no reason," and I'm forever grabbing my kids and telling them I love them.

However, she gave me all her talents, for which I'm thankful! She sewed all our clothes when we were growing up, then quit after I learned how. Her ability to play the piano and organ was overwhelming, and though I'll never be as good as she was, I can play. She taught me, and I can remember one of my piano "lessons" one day. It was the day I realized I'd never play as well as she could, no matter how hard I tried, so I told her that I quit. She just walked by and said, "Quit what?" I practiced another 25 minutes. Because of her, I can cook, can, quilt, survive, and charge head-on into just about anything (Thank you, Mom!).

My mother was involved in all the activities at church, and I suppose looking at that statement and putting it into context with some churches that we have today, it would seem rather a prideful statement. However, let me explain. My dad was the pastor of small town churches with small-town memberships, or even country churches with maybe 100 people. Being active in the life of the church was an everyday thing for us, and with mom playing the piano and organ and directing the choir, that was a lot of our week. Bible classes and Ladies Aid seemed to round out the rest of the church life for mom, and she thrived on all of it.

Fast forward to about 15 years ago. I was in nursing school and Mom and Dad came to visit us. She told me of some symptoms she was having in her left arm and leg (isn't it amazing how some people give you credit for knowing more than you do?), so I pulled out all my nursing books and found a gamut of diseases she could be having, but none of them were very nice, so I put the books back and told her she'd better keep her doctor's appointment when she went back home. Eventually, it was determined that she had osteoporosis, which wasn't so bad, all things considered. However, she continued to have "other" pains that weren't necessarily connected to osteoporosis, and she continued to have tests. We then found out she had Parkinson's disease. Not good.

Parkinson's is a nasty little disease that is called "progressive," which means it gets worse over time. It can either be rapid or slow in its progression, and it involves the brain cells, the neurons (part of the nervous system that controls the body's responses) and the production of Dopamine, a natural-occurring substance in the brain, which, when it's no longer produced in sufficient enough amounts, causes the brain cells to deteriorate. Thus, patients begin to lose their ability to walk, move, talk, think coherently – and they become totally dependent for everything. It is definitely not a fashionable disease to have.

When Mom first found out about the diagnosis, she was put on medications and seemed to do quite well. My sister thought many times that maybe they had misdiagnosed Mom, since the disease wasn't progressing much, and there are mimickers of Parkinson's. However, nothing definite ever came out of any other tests, so life went on for Mom and she continued doing what she could for a long as she could. She and Dad eventually moved to their own house – the first one they ever owned – after Dad retired from the ministry, and she was the organist for the church where Dad was asked to be an assistant "retired" pastor.

Then the crunch came and everything changed. My dad died, rather unexpectedly, I guess you could say, and my mom became this "other" person. Her stages of grieving never got past the anger stage – anger that Dad had died and left her to deal with everything on her own, and anger at God for taking her helpmeet of 40+ years. She never went through the rest of the grief process so she could get past the pain and start healing. My two brothers, my sister and I were all available to help her, in one way or the other, but none of us could get through the brick wall she was building. That was another thing my mother taught me – if you're going to do something, do it right. Her wall was solid. No chinks, no holes, no light at the end.

It was from this point on that her health became an issue. My sister and brother who live closest to her are both RN's; I'm an RN, and my other brother married an RN, so Mom couldn't have asked for any better help (if I do say so, myself) and support. However, she didn't want our help. She refused to move out of the house that she and Dad had built; she refused to let anyone live with her to take care of her; she just plain refused.

When she fell one night, broke her wrist and knocked herself out, she couldn't get up to answer the phone, and it was my sister trying to call her. Since Debbie knew mom couldn't go anywhere, especially at night, she continued to call the house, and finally asked the police in Mom's town to go and see if she were all right. That was when Debbie found out that Mom had fallen and was hurt.

She then called me to see what we should do, and for the first time in my whole life, I realized that Debbie and I were in the position of making decisions for our parent, rather than the other way around. Whoa! Wait a minute! The world had suddenly just gone haywire, and I was not ready for this! Talk about no instructions on raising kids – there sure aren't any books on parenting your parents! (Not in my library, anyway.)

Enter God. That was some rock dropped in the middle of our lives; it definitely got my attention, anyway! Once the shock wore off, and God got in on the conversation, the conversation went something like this:

"So, Judy, what do you think we should do?"

"Well, Debbie, she doesn't want to move out of the house, and we already know she won't stay with any of us for more than a day, then she wants to go home (I live 700 miles away to the south; Debbie lives 60 miles to the north). Think we could move her house to your back yard?"

"Funny, Judy."

We eventually decided that we'd talk to her and let her know that if she were to ever fall down and be unable to get up to get help, or if she broke another bone in her body, she would have to get some help with living. She could either live with one of her kids, or we'd make assisted living arrangements in a place we all liked. Boy, was that a tough conversation!

Judith Burhans

Over the next year, things went from bad to worse. Mom did go back home after her rehab with her wrist. Then, she fell and fractured her hip, and the rehab from that was long and painful. We moved her into a really nice assisted living apartment, and set up the room with all of her shelves, books, knick-knacks, rocking chair and pictures. While it wasn't home, it was homey and comfortable. Within two months, she was refusing to come out of her room and would lie in bed with the blinds closed. The staff called Debbie and told her Mom would have to leave because part of the agreement to live there was that the residents had to participate in meals down in the dining area. Mom refused to go.

From there, Debbie looked for nursing homes. She found one that was okay, as nursing homes go, though it wasn't nearly as nice as the assisted living place where she had been. A month after Mom moved into the nursing home, I went up to visit Debbie and Mom. We drove the four miles to the nursing home and Debbie told me to go ahead and get Mom from the cafeteria, since we had gotten there just as they were finishing lunch. So off I went, following the smells and sounds that led me straight to the cafeteria.

Now, this cafeteria wasn't that big – one glance in two directions was all it took to see everyone who was in there and what they were doing.

However, I couldn't find my mom. I looked again, and I still didn't see her. I went back to get Debbie to tell her I'd had no luck getting Mom, so she and I walked down to the cafeteria together. Debbie found this little, old, fragile-looking, gray-haired lady with her head tucked down into her chest, and wheeled her out of the cafeteria to me. The tears hit my eyes when I realized this was my mother, and I hadn't even recognized her. My heart broke and I felt so, so... miserable doesn't even begin to describe what I felt. I just looked at Debbie and saw the same pain in her eyes.

Okay, God, so You're not done with us, yet. HELP!

The result of that plea was that Debbie and her husband agreed to buy Mom a single-wide trailer, put the trailer in their backyard (they have a 30-acre farm), and connect the trailer to the house via a monitor communication system (Gerber nursery monitor and receiver). My mom gets the BEST care in the world, 24 hours a day, seven days a week. I have made the offer to Debbie that if she needs me for any reason, at any time of the year, she is to call me and I WILL be there.

I go up to visit when I can, although Mom does a lot of sleeping. She recognizes me when I do come, though, and tells me that I have to take her home, she doesn't want to stay there, any more, and I just listen. Debbie has brought Mom to me twice in the past few years so that she and her family can go away, and those experiences have both been mixed blessings. Mom's last visit to our house was quite recently. She can no longer move to walk on her own, nor can she feed herself any more. Debbie told me that Mom's diet was pretty skimpy as Mom was refusing to eat a lot of things that she needed, so Debbie brought me a bunch of eggs and some goat milk, gave me directions for some really fattening egg nog, which Mom would take, and told me to do the best I could with her diet.

Well, this was interesting. The first night there, she ate two bowls of ham and bean soup, which surprised Debbie, since she hadn't eaten that much in a long time. After Debbie was gone, I found that Mom would eat all the "different" meals one time, but if it came back as a leftover the next day, she didn't want it. Do you know how stubborn my mother's mouth is? The first time she refused to eat anything, I asked her if she wanted ice cream for dessert, and that got a positive response. I told her she had to eat her meal, first, then she could have dessert. Sound familiar?

The second time she refused to eat, even with the bribe of ice cream, I got in front of Mom's face so she could see me, and the conversation went like this:

"Mom, you have to eat this food."

"I'm not hungry."

"Mom, you haven't eaten all day – you have to eat. It's GOOD for you."

"I don't care."

"Mom, do you remember when I was little and you used to tell me I had to eat all my supper, whether I wanted to or not?"

"Yes, I guess so."

"Well, guess what, Mom? It's PAYBACK time!"

She laughed – a sound I hadn't heard in a long, long time; a sound I don't think she'd made in a long, long time.

Our two weeks together went by quickly, and soon Debbie and her family were back to get Mom. Mom asked me if she could stay with me and said she didn't want to go back with them, which, of course, made her leaving painful. However, I knew she was being well taken care of with Debbie, and I'm sure she forgot where she had been as soon as they headed down the road to go back home.

The hardest thing for me is looking at my mom, now, thinking about her as she was, and it's just about impossible to reconcile the difference. Her appearance, her abilities, her physical body – all are not how I want to remember her. I want her like she used to be – healthy, full of life, playing music, laughing, living with my dad, being my mother.

And then I have to remember the verse about being in the spittin' image of GOD, and I realize that the physical isn't what it's all about, anyway. It's the spirit and the soul that God gave to us, the image of GOD that transcends the physical pain and suffering and deterioration of the body. It brings the focus back to where I need to be and helps dry up the tears for me – this time. I pray it brings peace and comfort to my mom, too.

Judy Burhans

****

"So God created man in his own image, in the image of God he created him; male and female he created them." Genesis 1:27 NIV

MEET MY MOM AND MY DAD AND

MY MOM AND MY DAD

We have situations in today's society where children end up having more than one mother or father, either due to divorce and remarriage, the death of one parent or the other, or maybe the child is being taken away from the original family and placed in foster care and/or adopted due to circumstances beyond anyone's control. Sometimes the resulting "new" family is great, sometimes it leaves a lot to be desired. The following story is unique in that either the author of the story was a <u>very</u> difficult child to raise and it just took more people to get her through the growing up process, or God blessed her with just the right people at just the right moment to shape her into the person she is today. I think the pattern woven was just perfect.

JB

****

God comes to us in many ways, and for those people blessed with good parents, those parents can be the very best of God's tools. Maybe I needed more "working on" and thus needed more tools – but God has blessed me not with just two good parents, but with four – in fact, with even more than four!

My birth in 1944 came just three months after my father's death when his plane was shot down over World War II-torn Italy. My mother, a 20-year-old farm girl with only a high school education, suddenly found herself a widow and a parent. She had to figure out a way to raise a child and earn a living for the two of us, but she had no marketable skills. She returned to her native North Carolina, and her Aunt Loee and Uncle John took us in giving us a place to live and food to eat and love and protection — and there we stayed for eight years. God used these two warm, loving "parents" to provide everything Mother and I needed, and more.

During that time, my mother took a business course at a nearby two-year college, got a secretarial job at the power company, and started rebuilding her life. Meanwhile, I spent glorious childhood years as the treasured only child in a house full of adults. Aunt Loee and Uncle John had two married daughters, both of whom also lived there on the farm with their husbands. In addition, Aunt Loee and Uncle John had taken in my mother's sister when she was an infant and had raised her as their own, so until she married and moved away, she lived there too. A great big two-story farmhouse filled with eight adults and me. (Who—me? Spoiled? Surely you jest!). I roamed the farmland Uncle John owned, built playhouses in the pine thickets, and discovered my life-long love of reading. The whole community marveled at this throng of people, all living together in apparent harmony.

What lessons did God teach me through these folks? Well, one very obvious lesson is love, and another is generosity. I've never known people so filled with love or so generous with all they possessed as Aunt Loee and Uncle John. They were willing to take Mother and me in when we really had nowhere else to turn, and they'd have been willing for us to stay forever if that's what we had needed.

But God and my mother had other plans for us. When I was eight years old, Mother remarried, and we moved from the farm into our own little house in town. This stepfather that I acquired was, and still is, absolutely the best dad in the world. Since that day when I stood with him and my mother at the altar of the Presbyterian church, Daddy has been the rock I've leaned on. God has used him to teach me many, many things, such as patience and wisdom and honesty and perseverance. For example, Daddy has overcome a bad stuttering problem, and watching him live with that impediment and then get beyond it has taught me a great deal about perseverance as well as about how to relate to someone who is having that kind of problem. Together, Mother, Daddy, and I were a very happy family, and I had the bonus of being near Aunt Loee and Uncle John, so I still saw them almost every day. Again God was providing for me and forming me through loving, warm parents.

My mother continued working for most of my growing up years. One of the big lessons she wanted me to learn was that every woman needs a good education so that she can support herself, and during my teenage years, her primary goal was to make sure that I went to college. She worked hard to help me obtain a scholarship through the North Carolina Veterans Administration, and she was probably the proudest mom on campus the day she and Dad took me to college for my freshman year.

Little did I suspect that when she left me there that day, I would not be seeing her again in this life. Five days later, she died of a heart attack.

Words just don't cover what that felt like. My mother had been the center of my life for all of my 17 years; now my center was gone. She was gentle and good and sweet. She was the kindest person I've ever known. She was a true lady, who, I'm sure sometimes despaired of ever turning me into some semblance of a lady. She taught me the value of good manners in relating to people and the fact that a task worth doing is worth doing well. During the time just after her death, it was through Daddy that I learned how to trust God. God and Dad helped me return to college after Mother's funeral, and while I didn't excel that first year, Dad's lessons in perseverance helped me hang in there, and Mother's lessons about the value of education eventually helped me to earn my degree. I'd like to think that I learned some of her gentleness and kindness; at least I learned to appreciate those qualities in others.

Dad and I grew even closer after Mother's death than we had been before. Gradually, the paralyzing grief we had felt immediately after the death started to soften, and after some time, Daddy was ready for some sort of social life. Not long after Mother died, our next door neighbor, Eileen, had lost her husband, also to a heart attack, and it was at my urging that Dad first asked Eileen to go with him to a Christmas party at his club. The two of them seemed perfect for each other, and I eagerly watched and cheered from my college campus as they grew to love each other.

The spring of my junior year in college, Dad and Eileen were married. Eileen's daughter, Betsy, and I stood up with them, both of us thrilled about her new step-parent. Once again, God had given each of us a great family.

Judith Burhans

Eileen has now been my stepmother for nearly 37 years! She's wonderful! She really is. Through her, God has shown me more generosity, more patience, more kindness…and best of all, fun! She has an amazing joy for life that's contagious.

So has God used my "parents" to speak to me? Oh, yes, He has! I don't know that I've learned all these lessons modeled for me by Mother, Aunt Loee and Uncle John, Daddy, Eileen, and the others God has placed in my life, but one thing I have learned: God does provide. Just look at all the blessings He has provided for me – just when I needed them.

Kay Bradburn

****

"The LORD will guide you always; He will satisfy your needs in a sun-scorched land and will strengthen your frame. You will be like a well-watered garden, like a spring whose waters never fail." (Isaiah 58:11, NIV)

PART VI

KNOCKS, WHISPERS AND OTHER ATTENTION GETTERS

God does work in mysterious ways and for mysterious purposes, or so it seems. Sometimes, we are given the wisdom to see the pattern that is occurring; sometimes, we wonder until we die what something meant, why something happened, or even what it was that did happen! God gives us "tools" to use that will help us as we either wander aimlessly, trudge along with hang-dog faces, or stride in confidence through life. Prayer, friends, His Word and His promises are only some of the things He offers us daily; His blessings are unending when we hear the knock-knock and listen to how He wants us to respond to those opportunities. We've seen many examples of some Knock-Knocks that God has used, and we've seen how other women have answered the knocks.

The following stories, appropriately enough, are the final ones of the book. Some deal with the last knock-knocks that are heard before eternity; some deal with knocks that bring about a conclusion to a chapter in life. However, through God's promise of strength to us, and with our faith that He WILL give us what we need, we can – and do! – find joy in all things.

Judith Burhans

"Peace I leave with you; My peace I give you. I do not give to you as the world gives. Do not let your hearts be troubled and do not be afraid (John 14:27, NIV); *and Lo, I am with you ALWAYS, even to the end of the earth."* (Matthew 28:20, NIV)

JB

****

FULL CIRCLE

My early years were full of music, as my father was a musician. In addition to five city and high school orchestras and bands, he taught private violin lessons and I followed him everywhere. I loved him so much – he taught me to play the violin and we played together. He also was the one who wiped my tears away, took me to the beach to pick up shells and talk about their beauty, made me slow down to watch the birds, the sunsets. I learned from him that music brought me joy and peace.

Daddy left us when I was about eight years old and with his departure went the music as well as any joy in our home. I still played the violin, but it was not the same and I became a reader of many, many books over the next few years. My violin was stolen when I was about 14 years old and with that loss, my music was gone completely. I felt that part of my life was over and closed the door.

How can it be that someone that loved music so much could live without it? We walk in many different directions in our journey and mine took me to a marriage of 34 years with a man who didn't understand the soul's need for music, shells, birds, and sunsets. What did come from this marriage were three beautiful girls who I loved, and still love, more than life.

During the year before my divorce, I began to seek our Lord in a personal way, found a church that took me in and nurtured me. In the year following my divorce, I began to desire to play again. That was about nine years ago.

I have learned in the past nine years what God meant us to do with music — and that is to praise and worship Him. I have been given a gift of harmony with no notes to read from — a passion to play with others to Him and for Him. I have learned that a music leader's role is to enable others to worship and praise Him in song and melody — and that the angels join us when we worship Him.

God has given me special people to play with. Sandy, who plays with me in our worship team, breathes with me now. God joins as one in Him when we play together. Sometimes I think of the young girl who thought her music was over, forever. And I thank Him for my life, and for the joy in praising Him, and for the honor in bringing His beautiful music to others.

I see now that none of us knows what tomorrow brings. At any given moment in our lives, time will take unexpected turns, it will stand still or it will rush forward. I also see that our Lord walks with us in all of our steps. He will catch us if we stumble, He will give us tools to go on, and He will bring us joy.

Susan Sadler

****

"By day the LORD directs His love,

at night His song is with me,

a prayer to the God of my life." (Psalm 42:8 NIV)

Judith Burhans

SILENCE ISN'T ALWAYS GOLDEN

Confrontations are painful for most people, especially if the confrontation involves a loved one and his or her spirituality – or lack thereof. Even those of us who can talk a mile a minute about anything, and in any situation, may find no words available at all when it comes to matters of the heart and soul – and salvation. The silence is pretty deep. What then?

JB

****

I grew up in a house full of loving, good people—a couple of aunts, an uncle, some adult cousins—and my mother saw to it that I attended church regularly. But my favorite of the cousins (I'll call him Sam) was not a churchgoer. In fact, he had a pretty bad problem with binge drinking, and every sentence he spoke was salted with curse words. He had terrible nightmares and would wake up sometimes screaming.

Sam had a kind and generous heart, but he didn't have the Lord in his life, as far as I could tell. When I was a child, it really bothered me that Sam didn't seem to care about God, and I asked my mother about it. She told me that people show God in their lives in different ways and that it wasn't up to me to judge whether or not Sam was "in God's good graces." Still, it bothered me, and as I heard more at church about sharing the faith and witnessing for the Lord, I began to feel a burden to talk to Sam about God…but somehow, I couldn't make myself do it.

"Please God, help me to talk to him about you. Give me the courage." But the years passed, and I still lacked the courage to speak.

As I passed from my teens into young adulthood, I still had not talked to Sam, even though he had been diagnosed with lung cancer. Even after his surgery to remove one lung, I could not figure out how to broach the subject. Meanwhile, I had finished college, married, moved to another state, and started a family. I still prayed daily for Sam, but now my prayer became, "Please, God, send someone to touch Sam's heart…or help me to do it."

The time came when Sam's body no longer could fight the cancer, and he died. Added to my sadness over his death was an enormous feeling of guilt that I never had talked to him about God. With a very heavy heart, I returned to my hometown to attend Sam's funeral, which was held at the church the rest of the family attended. This church had gotten a new minister within the last year and I had not met him. He did a fine job of

Judith Burhans

conducting the ceremony, but as the family would say, I was "taking it hard." Maybe that's the reason this young minister sought me out after the funeral.

It was this minister whom God used to deliver to me the joyful answer for all those years of prayers on Sam's behalf. As he shook my hand, he looked into my face and said, "I feel I need to tell you something. Sam and I shared many hours together during his last weeks in the hospital. I want you to know that during that time, he accepted the Lord into his life, and before he died he was completely ready to meet the Lord in Heaven."

Kay Bradburn

****

"...the Spirit helps us in our weakness. We do not know what we ought to pray for, but the Spirit himself intercedes for us with groans that words cannot express." (Romans 8:26, NIV)

WHEN FAITH IS BRUISED

God has never promised us a rose garden; that's a human fallacy. He has never promised us that we would never suffer or have pain; that's either dreaming or death. He has promised us, though, the strength to get through the hard times; the support we need for the asking (and believing); His hand to protect us when our heart has broken; and His whisper of love and faithfulness in the darkness. His plan for us is in place, and we can find comfort in knowing that He only has the very, very best waiting for us, no matter what.

JB

****

"God is sovereign." "God is omniscient." "God is all-powerful." YES, and even, "Jesus loves me." As a Christian, these are all truths I believe. Lately, they are things I repeat in my head like a chant, but struggle with in my heart. It is hard to admit, and makes me question the sincerity of my Christianity, but my faith has been bruised.

I have led a blessed life. It has by no means been an easy life, but it has certainly been blessed. I have dealt with many a blow in the boxing match of life, but by the grace and mercy of God, I have not been knocked down. Until now.

My husband and I, like many other couples these days, have been diagnosed with an infertility problem. This diagnosis came after two miscarriages and a long struggle to become pregnant. After many prayers and some fertility treatment, we became pregnant. We have a beautiful little girl and a life lesson in the preciousness of life. When she was 14 months old, we were excited to find out that we were expecting again - and no fertility drugs were necessary. Life was good; life was moving along.

The pregnancy went very smoothly. By Christmas time, I was six months along and my little girl understood that there was a baby in mommy's tummy. She would take little ornaments from the Christmas tree and hold them up to my stomach to show the baby. It is amazing to me how much little ones observe and take in, even though they may not understand everything.

The due date was March 7. Of course, hardly anyone delivers on her due date. I was hoping the baby would come on my birthday, March 11. A couple of days before March 7, I woke up to go to the bathroom and had a gush of blood release from my uterus. The bleeding was isolated to the gush and did not continue. My doctor thought everything seemed normal, especially knowing the baby was getting bigger. On March 9, around 10:00 o'clock at night, my water broke. This had happened with my daughter, but this time there was a lot of blood. We made it to the hospital by 11:00 PM. By 3:00 AM, I was ready to deliver. Near the end of delivery, the baby was under distress and the last five minutes, there was a flurry to get the baby out. William David (named after my father-in-law and my husband) was born at 3:17 AM. He was placed on my stomach and as I looked at him, I was confused. He was blue, still, and quiet. Was this normal?

Everything was so quiet. No one said anything. The doctor and nurses whisked Will away to clear out his mouth and sinuses and clean him up. My husband and I just looked at each other, not understanding. Our daughter had been blessed with a loud cry from the moment she was born. Why wasn't he crying?

The neonatologist soon arrived and let us know that our baby was not responsive. He was not breathing, and they needed to monitor him in the intensive nursery care unit. I was stitched up, cleaned up and assigned a room. It wasn't until later that I found out that I was not on the maternity ward. A special card was placed on our door to let the staff know that all was not well. My husband and I prayed that God would take care of our precious gift from Him. We asked that all would be well and we would be able to go home with our son very soon.

My husband had the ominous task of calling family and announcing our news. Prayers were lifted up. He was also the one who took our family up to see the newest member of the clan. He saw Will hooked up to tubes laying in a bassinet, being monitored constantly. When we went to sleep the night of the March 10, things were looking up. I knew God was going to make everything just fine and our prayers would be answered.

The next morning, my birthday, I awoke early. I put my robe on and woke up David. I was ready to go see Will. We called up to NICU to make sure it was okay to visit. The nurse said that the neonatologist wanted to come down to see us before we went up. Soon thereafter, we found out from the doctor that Will had not done well during the night. More tests were being run and Little Will was receiving his second donation of blood. This was not a good sign, and according to our doctor, David and I were to begin preparing ourselves to lose Will. We called our family to come. At 10:00 AM, we received a call to come on to the floor; not to introduce our families to our newborn son, but to say our good-byes. Our prayers had been answered.

We buried our son the following Sunday. People – friends, co-workers, acquaintances, family – all came to support us and to mourn with us. The number of people who shared our grief with us was overwhelming, and continues to be a source of amazement to me. The service was beautiful. My husband had made a cradle, which we placed up at the altar.

On a follow-up appointment with the neonatologist, we were told that no genetic problems had been uncovered that would discourage us from having other children. Will was a healthy 8-plus pound baby, but the problem was with the umbilical cord's attachment to the placenta. As Will was delivered, the umbilical cord pulled away from the placenta, depriving him of blood and oxygen long enough to send him into shock. His little body just couldn't recover.

It has almost been two years, and it is still unbelievable and numbing to recount this experience. I continue to mourn, but time does help. My heart winces when people talk about birthdays. It was bad enough that we lost Will, but why did it have to be on my birthday? Is this what a loving God allows to happen to His children? We prayed what any parent would pray,

Judith Burhans

"Please make our child well and let us take him home!" Weren't we specific enough? Maybe we should have mentioned our address to differentiate from our heavenly home. It is not like we were asking for a red sports car, fully loaded. We were asking for our child's life. Isn't that what we should do? Never has 'No' been such a hard answer to hear and live with.

My head knows that God is sovereign. My mind holds on to that fact. My head knows that God is loving and all-powerful. My head knows that I am His child through the precious gift of His Son, Jesus the Christ, whom he gave up <u>willingly</u>, for me and you, all of us sinners. I am a new creation, the old is gone. I know that He is working in me through all this misery to give me wisdom, compassion, kindness, and gentleness. My head knows these things and clings to them for life until my heart stops aching from the hurt of the blow.

My faith has been bruised. I have been knocked down, but not knocked out. I am just nursing some hard blows knowing that as I heal, I will be even stronger - by the grace of God and to His glory.

Karen Zecher

****

"He spreads out the northern skies over empty space; He suspends the earth over nothing. He wraps up the waters in His clouds, yet the clouds do not burst under their weight. He covers the face of the full moon, spreading His clouds over it. He marks out the horizon on the face of the waters for a boundary between light and darkness...And these are but the outer fringe of His works; how faint the whisper we hear of Him! Who then can understand the thunder of His power?" (Job 26:7-10, 14, NIV)

Judith Burhans

AND GOD SAID...

A few stories introduce themselves, and I think this is one of those.

JB

****

A first grade teacher once told me that a little boy in her class, Steven, was a bit of a handful, always talking, seldom sitting still long enough to get his work done. Finally, when all other measures had failed to convince Steven to sit still and do his work, she asked the principal to have a word with him. The principal came to the classroom early one school morning and had a talk with Steven about the importance of obeying his teacher and working hard. In parting, the principal said, "I'm going to be checking on you from time to time to see if you're being a good boy, Steven."

That afternoon, the principal got caught up in other duties and didn't have time to return to Steven's classroom, but he wanted to follow through on his promise to the little boy. So he turned to the school intercom, flipped open the switch that would allow his voice to be heard in Steven's classroom, and spoke into the microphone.

Meanwhile, in the classroom, the children were laboring over a worksheet the teacher had given them, when suddenly the principal's voice filled the room: "Steven, are you doing your work?" the deep voice demanded.

Gasping and opening his eyes wide with awe, Steven whispered, "God's talking to me!"

****

Many times in my life, I am like Steven – I need a little talking to – and God always comes through with just the right words. Sometimes those words come through a song or a statement in my pastor's sermon; sometimes it's a scripture verse or a passage in something else I'm reading. Sometimes God speaks to me through some natural phenomenon, like the calming sound of rain on the nice snug roof over my head or the merry sparkle of sunlight dancing on ripples in the pond beside my house. But quite often, God encourages me through the words of a friend, or even the words of someone I don't know.

Our son, Chuck, was not an easy teenager. He was fearless and often foolish in the choices he made, and his father and I prayed every day that

Judith Burhans

God would just help Chuck to survive growing up, that God would help us get him through high school. I think that as a high school student, Chuck tried every available substance, legal or illegal, and many were the days he cut classes to go "hang" with his friends down at the river, so of course his grades were deplorable. I was frequently in despair. It seemed to me (although it may not have really been so) that all my friends' sons were making good grades; were planning for college, looked clean cut, behaved themselves like model citizens. I would pray and pray, but most of the time, I wasn't really letting go of my worry. Most of the time, I really needed some reassurance…or a talking to.

On one such morning during my son's high school career, I answered the phone, and my heart sank when I learned that the caller was Chuck's math teacher. I had introduced myself to her at a PTA meeting, but she and I didn't really know each other. She said, "I'm calling you because I was sitting here thinking about Chuck, and I suddenly felt I should tell you something."

"Oh, no!" I thought. "What's he done now?" I said, "Oh, I'm so sorry if he has disrupted your class!"

"No," she said. "He's a perfect gentleman, the best behaved student I have – never causes any trouble at all – just sits back there and reads. Of course, he's getting a 'D' this six weeks in my class, but he's never any trouble at all. But I watch him, and I see what he's up to. I was just thinking about how worried you must be about him, and I wanted to tell you to stop worrying. Chuck's going to be okay. I've been a teacher for a lot of years, and I'm pretty good about judging which kids are the truly bad ones and which ones are just going through a phase."

"Oh," I let out the breath I hadn't realized I'd been holding. "Thank you! Do you really think so?"

"Yes, I do," she said firmly. "He's going to turn himself around one of these days. I can tell he's been raised right, and he's going to do a turn-around when you're least expecting it.'

I thanked her profusely for calling and hung up the phone. And then before going on with my day with a much lighter heart, I thanked God for sending those words to me. He did, you know. Why else would this woman who barely knew who I was, take time out of her busy day to call and reassure me? God must have prompted that call and those reassuring words. Like Steven, I could say with awe, "God's talking to me!"

Kay Bradburn

****

Judith Burhans

"Be still, and know that I am God; I will be exalted among the nations, I will be exalted in the earth." (Psalm 46:10, NIV)

The Knock-Knock Book
If I Hear God Knocking, Do You Think I Should Answer?

LET GO - LET GOD

The first time I saw this little expression, it was on a counted cross stitch piece of material and hanging on somebody's fridge. My first thought, I think, was, "How cute!" My second thought was, "Just one letter different in both lines, not too tough," and then I really READ it, and I thought, "WOW!" Easy to cross stitch, hard to live!

I have truly let go and let God twice in my life – well, twice that it made a really significant difference in how I handled the situation – and the response I got from those around me was, "Don't you care?"

JB

****

Too many years ago to count (or to count and want to tell!), my dad had a massive heart attack. At the time, I was living in Kansas. Debbie, my sister, was going to nursing school in a town about 2-1/2 hours away from me, and it was the middle of winter for the northern part of the country. At 3:00 PM, I got a call from one of the members at the congregation where dad was the pastor, and from there, the rest of the day is a blur. I remember calling Debbie and making arrangements to drive down to get her, drive back up to the interstate, and drive to Indiana, all in the few hours before Dad's surgery was scheduled the next morning.

To make a long story short, comparatively speaking, we got out of Kansas at some point, but it was dark and cold; snow was in the forecast for all the states through which we had to drive. Debbie couldn't drive because her glasses were broken, which meant I got to claim the driver's seat for the whole trip. Look out, I-70! Here we come!

As we passed Kansas City - Missouri or Kansas, I'm not sure, the one with the airport – we both looked to the left and thought about how much quicker we'd get to Indiana if we could just fly there, but money was a factor for both of us, so we continued on our way.

Around 3:00 AM, the time of darkest thoughts while driving, I think, I began to remember all these days in my life where Dad was the main character, my Hero. Debbie and I talked and talked. Sometimes our memories collided, sometimes they didn't because of our age span, but we could put together the picture of Dad and share it with each other.

By the time the sun was beginning to shine, we were finally getting close enough to home to begin to wonder what was in store for us, now. The Unknown was huge in this instance, and very easily could have become quite powerful and overwhelming. At 9:00 AM, we made it to the house in town where I dropped off Debbie, then went on to the hospital by myself.

That's when I found out what the other ingredient was that was needed for total panic – being Alone with the Great Unknown! Wow! I still had nine miles to go before I got to the hospital, and since this was the era before cell phones and satellite tracking devices, I had no way of knowing what was going on in that hospital, or if Dad were even still in the land of the living. We hadn't stopped during the night to call and get any updates; we were more concerned about making good time and just getting there! So, when I realized that we didn't know anything, the tears began, but then with the tears, there was this combination of fear, for sure, and something else – not quite an anger, but something that made the tears not tears of pity, but rather tears of disbelief, I think.

Now, remember, I had nine miles to drive down a country road, the back way to the hospital. The glare from the snow was blinding, I had been sleep deprived for at least 30 hours, and here's what you would have heard if you'd been with me in that car:

"OK, God, I don't think You need him, You know? Look at all those people You've already got up there with You. There's Grandma and

Grandpa Vavra, Peter and Paul, Martin Luther, and probably Tennessee Ernie Ford. You've got angels everywhere, and You've got all the company You need right now. You told us that we wouldn't die until it was our time. Well, God, it's not Dad's time, yet. Look at what's happening to our church's Synod! You need pastors here like Dad, pastors who will preach Your Word like it's supposed to be preached – in all its purity. My Dad does that. He doesn't take passages from the Bible and say, 'Well, God really didn't mean that, it's just a figure of speech.' Oh, no, God, Dad would never change Your Word like some other pastors are doing, right now. I know we all have to die, God, but I really don't think it's his time, is it? Besides that, I need him around for a while longer because he still has things to teach me, too. Okay, God?"

I pulled into the parking lot of the hospital, sat there a few minutes more, just to make sure the last of my conversation had settled down, and to hear God reply – if He were going to reply. It's a good thing I was sitting, too, because this peace came down and filled me so full, I knew I had my answer! I was so excited, I forgot why I was at the hospital. Needless to say, when I got into the hospital, my mother thought my smile was very inappropriate, and it probably was. She was totally worried and had been crying, both of which were more "appropriate," I'm sure, considering the circumstances, but I had this peace!

It was too late to see Dad before he went to pre-surgery, so Mom and I went to the waiting room to wait (obviously). We sat down and she asked me if I weren't worried about my father - this was a serious surgery and he was in bad shape. I looked at Mom across the small waiting room, pulled my knees up under my chin and wrapped my arms around my legs and said, "Mom, you're not going to believe this, but Dad's going to be just fine." And with those profound words of wisdom, I fell asleep; totally, absolutely, missed-the-whole-time-in-surgery, completely asleep.

Five hours and Dad's-in-the-recovery-room later, I woke up and Mom's next words to me were, "Well, it's a little late, now. Your father's out of surgery and in recovery." The implication was that I hadn't worried; therefore, I didn't care. The truth was, I HAD LET GO so I didn't have to do the worrying! It was wonderful!

Fifteen years later (and yes, Dad slew satanical dragons and preached the Word of Truth and of God), I once again got a call that Dad was back in the hospital. Once again, the weather was rotten - in the South, this time - and I had to spend the night in Kentucky because of the ice that was closing down the interstate from Alabama. Once again, I alone drove the distance, and once again, I stopped at the main house before heading to the hospital. The phone was ringing in the house, this time, and it was my brother-in-law, telling me I'd better get up there in a hurry if I wanted to talk to Dad before it was too late. Once again, I drove the last few miles and had another conversation with God, but this one was a lot different than the first one.

"OK, God, I'm back, and it's my Dad I'm here for, again. I remember that we've had this conversation before, but this time, God, let me just thank You for the past 15 years that You've given him, and that You've given me to spend more time with him. Thank You so much! I guess he's done what You wanted him to do, hasn't he? He's completed his weave in Your pattern and plan, so I guess it would be really selfish of me to ask for more. Do You really want him there, now? Right now? Will he get to see Grandpa Coull and his own mom and dad? Is he going to be singing with the saints - and singing bass? And seeing You? He's going to be happy, isn't he, God? He was a good servant for You, You know. Just let me talk to him before You take him, OK?"

This time, Dad wasn't in surgery; there was nothing they could do for him. My sister and her family where there, my other brother was there, and I was the "fresh" one to arrive. Dad was not conscious when I got there, and Debbie said he'd been talking until about 4:00 PM; it was now going onto 5:00 PM. After a few minutes there and watching the monitor, looking at Dad, and praying, I decided it might be a good thing to call my brother who wasn't there yet, since he had to come from Nebraska. Then I called my friend, one of those precious treasures that God gives us for times just like these, and I told her I didn't think God was going to answer me like He had before. I told her I thought God's answer this time was, "I'm taking Him with Me; he's ready." Angie told me that was really okay, too, that God would do what was best for His child. I knew that; it was just hard to hear.

By 10:30 that night, everyone had gone to different places for a rest period. Mom had been at the hospital most of the time that Dad had been there, and she needed to lie down. Debbie and I were the only two left, and once again, we talked about Dad and our memories. We talked *to* Dad and told him all our fears and hopes that even now, he might come back to us, because really, how could we deal with him being gone? We all needed him, didn't he know?

Then it hit me, right in the attention-getting place of the brain – Dad didn't need to hear this from us! He was the one dying, he was the one going through the hard part, and we were bemoaning the fact that we needed him to hang in there and come back to us. How human! So I told Debbie I thought we needed to let Dad go and let him hear something that would help him, that whatever he heard before he died, it didn't need to be, "Don't go, Dad!"

And once again, God was there. Just right there in that room. Debbie and I held hands across Dad's bed. Each of us took one of his hands in ours and held it and let the tears flow. I asked Debbie if she remembered the 23rd Psalm, and she said probably most of it, so together, we spoke the 23rd Psalm together. What she didn't know, I did, and what I had forgotten, she remembered. Dad was probably wondering how either of us could have forgotten any of the words, as often as we had to say it in Confirmation classes! We did a resounding job of the Lord's Prayer, though, and then we sang <u>all</u> <u>eight</u> verses of "I Know That My Redeemer Lives," Dad's favorite (well, right up there with all his other "favorite" hymns!) hymn.

And here comes the really, really cool part. Are you ready? As soon as we sang that last verse of "I Know That My Redeemer Lives," there was about a 30-second period of time, and then we both heard the sound of a huge breath going out, and he was gone. The respirator was still going, but

Debbie and I both knew, in the same instant, that Dad was gone. He had gone with God, and we had let him go.

As I write this last chapter of the book, I'm also writing on the last day of my mother's life. I found out earlier this evening that Mom had died, too, but for her, I wasn't there. Tomorrow, I'll make one more drive, and tomorrow I'll deal with letting go, again. For tonight, I'm in the presence of God and His love.

Judy Burhans

****

"The LORD bless you and keep you; the LORD make His face shine upon you and be gracious unto you; the LORD lift up His countenance upon you, and give you peace." (Numbers 6:24-26, NKJV) AMEN!

ABOUT THE AUTHOR/CO-AUTHORS:

Judy Burhans is the mother of ten (at last count, including foster and adopted children) whose greatest fear is running out of things to do; hence, the book.

Kay Bradburn is the mother of two grown children and works at the University of Alabama, teaching technical writing to college students. She enjoys "nesting" in her country home and watching the squirrels watching her.

Sandra McCutcheon is also the mother of two grown children and spends her waking hours looking at insurance figures. Music and being "in charge" of something fill her time; her hippie days are over – maybe.

Karen Zecher, mother of one (soon to be two), is a full-time mother and wife. She spends many hours teaching her daughter rhymes and songs; wait, maybe it's the other way around.

Susan Sadler is the mother of three grown women, four growing grandchildren, and most recently, one new great-grandchild! Her passions include playing the violin like a violin is supposed to be played.

All of these women make their homes in the Huntsville/Madison, Alabama, area, which is known primarily for its high-tech engineers, space and rockets. It is now known for five women who have heard God knock in their lives and decided to "answer" the door. Like the scientists who launch their rockets into outer space, we are stepping out in faith that some of our stories will hit a target in your heart and make you feel the power and love of God in your life.

To God be the glory – great things He has done!